P9-DBX-016

LINGERIE
& SLEEPWEAR

24 original designs
you can make yourself

Edited by Jack Angell

St. Martin's Press
New York

Photographs: Neil Menneer
Instructions: Eileen Lowcock
Design co-ordinator: Jayne Stewart
Patterns and cutting layouts: Ian Kirkwood
Line drawings: Terry Evans
Photography on location at the
Park Lane Hotel, London

Book design: Mike Head
Assistant editor: Pam Darlaston
Production: Edward Allhusen

Library of Congress Catalog Card Number
81-52169
ISBN 0–312–48698–7 (Millboard edition)
ISBN 0–312–48699–5 (Paperback edition)

© David & Charles (Publishers) Ltd 1981

All rights reserved. No part of this
publication may be reproduced, stored
in a retrieval system, or transmitted,
in any form or by any means, electronic,
mechanical, photocopying, recording or
otherwise, without the prior permission
of David & Charles (Publishers) Limited.

Typeset by Keyspools Ltd,
Golborne, Lancs,
and printed in The Netherlands
by Royal Smeets Offset Weert
for David & Charles (Publishers) Limited
Brunel House   Newton Abbot   Devon

First published in the United States of
America in 1982
This editon published by
St. Martin's Press, Inc., 175 Fifth Avenue,
New York, N.Y. 10010

Contents

Introduction 4

Nightshirt 5
Designer: Sandra Dodds   Model: Chanell

Nightie & négligé 10
Designer: Christine Browett   Model: Diane

Silk pyjamas 17
Designer: Sandra Dodds   Model: Rebecca

Winter nightdress 22
Designer: Sandra Dodds   Model: Rocky

Quilted bedjacket 28
Designer: Jayne Stewart   Model: Diane

Sleepsuit & jacket 34
Designer: Christine Browett   Model: Rebecca

Knitted vest & knickers 40
Designer: Carole Gabara   Model: Rocky

Floral pyjamas 44
Designer: Christine Browett   Model: Rocky

Stretch terry sleepsuit 51
Designer: Sandra Dodds   Model: Diane

Housedress 55
Designer: Tenny Wong   Model: Rebecca

Kimono 60
Designer: Margaret Leach   Model: Chanell

Négligé 63
Designer: Annette O'Toole   Model: Rebecca

Tracksuit 69
Designer: Imogen Evans   Model: Chanell

Terry cloth bathrobe 74
Designer: Margaret Leach   Model: Debbie

Summer dressing-gown 79
Designer: Tenny Wong   Model: Debbie

Quilted dressing-gown 84
Designer: Imogen Evans   Model: Chanell

Tap pants & bra 90
Designer: Christine Browett   Model: Rocky

Camisole 95
Designer: Jayne Stewart   Model: Debbie

Petticoat 99
Designer: Sandra Dodds   Model: Rebecca

Knitted teddy 102
Designer: Carole Gabara   Model: Debbie

Knitted bedjacket 105
Designer: Carole Gabara   Model: Chanell

Silk teddy 108
Designer: Christine Browett   Model: Diane

Lace bra & briefs 114
Designer: Christine Browett   Model: Rocky

Waist slip 118
Designer: Jayne Stewart   Model: Debbie

Dressmaking techniques 121

Introduction

The idea for *Lingerie* came as a result of answering a direct mail advertisement for a birthday present for my wife. It was a nightdress made by a well-known designer and when it arrived it was all that the copywriter had promised – except that it did not fit. Apparently all women are at least 5ft 6in tall in the world of fashion but Alice is only 5ft 2in. The choice was either to undertake difficult alterations because of the lace trim, or to take the risk of accidents in the home.

It appeared to my untutored eye that this expensive nightdress would be relatively simple to make but a study of the books available revealed that there was a need for imaginative designs, beautifully modelled and photographed, with clear simple instructions on how to make them.

And so ... a book was born.

A team of talented young designers was commissioned to submit their ideas for a wide range of lingerie, nightwear and playsuits and the sketches selected were made-up using techniques and materials available to the home seamstress. The final choice was an extremely difficult one and Jayne Stewart proved to be an invaluable aide in selecting designs and co-ordinating the work of the many people involved.

Neil Menneer, the young photographer, lived up to his promise in every way and the Park Lane Hotel, London, went to a great deal of trouble to provide the suites and other settings for the photographs. The task of writing instructions for making-up other people's ideas is no easy one and I was extremely fortunate to have Eileen Lowcock to take on the fastidious detail.

To everyone else who contributed – thank you.

Anyone with basic dressmaking experience will be able to tackle any of the garments without difficulty and the absolute beginner will find the chapter on basic techniques an invaluable aid. The superb colour photography is supported by designers' sketches with samples of the materials used. In addition to the step-by-step instructions, the comprehensive line drawings, patterns and cutting layouts will ensure a completely successful result. A chart enables alterations to size to be undertaken without difficulty and alternative materials may be chosen should a different weight or less expensive fabric be preferred.

I make no apology for including three charming knitted patterns which complement those requiring needle and thread.

JACK ANGELL

Nightshirt

*Made in striped winceyette, this nightshirt will keep
you cosy on the coldest night. For summer wear you
could make it in a cool cotton seersucker.*

Materials
2.5m (2¼yd) of 115cm (45in) wide fabric
Iron-on woven interfacing for front bands and
collar
7 buttons 1.5cm (⅝in)
sewing thread to match fabric
squared paper for pattern

Measurements
The pattern is given in size 12, for measurements
see chart on page 123.

To make pattern
Draw up the pattern to scale from the graph
pattern given here. One square represents 5cm
(2in).

To adapt pattern
For size 10, cut away 1.3cm (½in) from front and
back side edges and underarm edges on sleeves.
For size 14, alter in the same places but add
amounts.

To cut out
No seam allowance is included on the pattern.
When cutting out add 1.5cm (⅝in) to all seam
edges including hem edge and 2cm (¾in) to
sleeve-hem edges.
Pin pattern pieces to fabric following the cutting
layout and cut out.
Transfer all pattern markings.

To make nightshirt
1   Iron on interfacing up to the fold line on
wrong side of front bands and collar.
2   With right sides together, tack and stitch
across both short ends of each front band.
3   With right sides together, tack and stitch
front bands to shirt fronts, leaving one edge free.
Snip seam allowance on shirt fronts to end of
stitching. Turn under seam allowance on raw
edge of band and slipstitch to line of stitching.
See diagram 1. Press flat.
4   On the pocket facing edge, turn under 6mm
(¼in) and tack. With right sides together, fold
pocket facing back and stitch short ends. Trim
seam allowance and cut across corners. *See
diagram 2.* Turn pocket to right side. Tack close
to stitched and folded edges. Hem pocket facing
to pocket. Turn seam allowance to wrong side

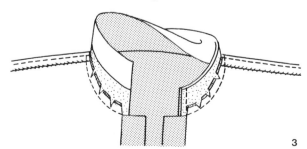

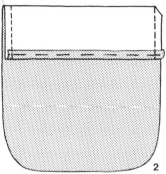

on remaining edges and tack. Press flat.
Tack and stitch pocket to shirt right front as
indicated on pattern.
5   With right sides together, tack and stitch the
fronts to the back at shoulder seams. Press seam
towards the front and neaten the raw edges
together by hand or machine overcasting. On
right side, top stitch close to seamline and then
6mm (¼in) away to hold seam allowance in
place. Press flat.
6   With right sides together, tack and stitch the
interfaced edge of the collar to the neck edge.
Press the seam towards the collar and notch the
seam allowance where necessary.
With right sides together, tack and stitch the
short ends of the collar. *See diagram 3.* Trim the
seam allowance and turn collar to right side.
Tack close to stitched edges and fold. Turn under

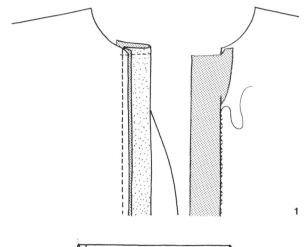

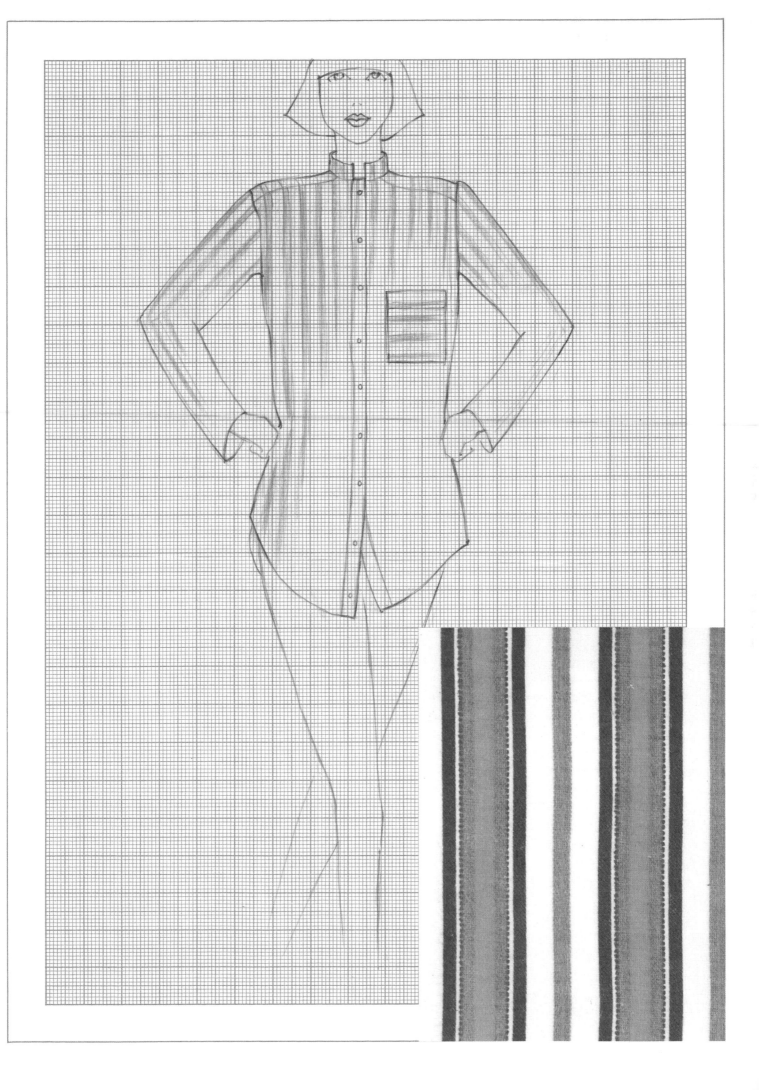

seam allowance on free edge of collar and slipstitch it to the line of stitching. Press flat.

7 With right sides together, matching circle to shoulder seam and notches, tack and stitch the sleeves into the armholes. *See diagram 4.* Press seam towards sleeve and neaten the raw edges together. On the right side, top stitch close to the seamline.

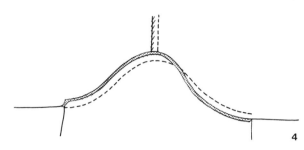

4

8 Neaten the raw edges of side seams, underarm seams and garment hem by turning under 3mm ($\frac{1}{8}$in) and machine stitching. Press all edges flat.

9 With right sides together, tack and stitch each underarm and side seam from sleeve-hem edge to notch at side seam. Press seam open.

10 Turn up garment hem and sew in place by hand hemming. Press flat.

11 At sleeve-hem edge, turn under 6mm ($\frac{1}{4}$in) and then a further 1.3cm ($\frac{1}{2}$in). Machine hem in place. Press flat.

12 On right side, top stitch 6mm ($\frac{1}{4}$in) in from front-band, collar and hem edges.

13 On right-front band work seven buttonholes as indicated on the pattern. On left-hand band, sew buttons to correspond.

fold

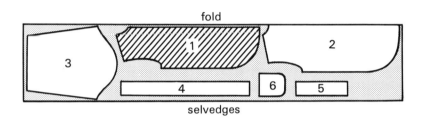

selvedges

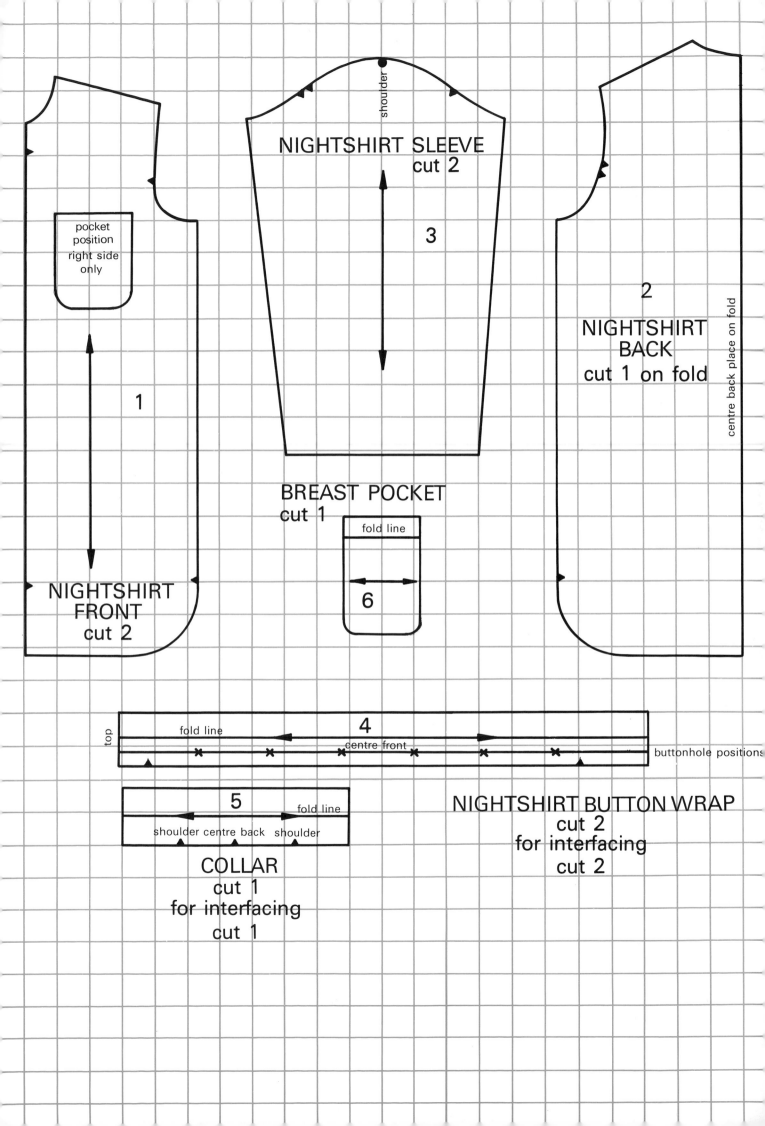

NIGHTSHIRT SLEEVE
cut 2

shoulder

3

2

NIGHTSHIRT
BACK
cut 1 on fold

centre back place on fold

pocket
position
right side
only

1

NIGHTSHIRT
FRONT
cut 2

BREAST POCKET
cut 1

fold line

6

top

fold line

4

centre front

buttonhole positions

5

fold line

shoulder   centre back   shoulder

COLLAR
cut 1
for interfacing
cut 1

NIGHTSHIRT BUTTON WRAP
cut 2
for interfacing
cut 2

Nightie & négligé

Daintily trimmed with lace, this nightdress and négligé are made in a fine polyester crêpe-de-chine. The nightdress has a pretty shaped top but otherwise is quite plain, and the whole ensemble is simple to make.

Materials
4m (4⅓yd) of 115cm (45in) wide jaquard polyester fabric
5.7m (6¼yd) of 4cm (1½in) wide scallop-edged nylon lace
1.3m (1½yd) of 6mm (¼in) wide satin ribbon
sewing thread to match fabric
squared paper for patterns

Measurements
The pattern is given in size 12, for measurements see chart on page 123.

To make pattern
Draw up the pattern to scale from the graph pattern given here. One square represents 5cm (2in).

To adapt pattern
For size 10, cut away 1.3cm (½in) from nightdress front and back side-seam edges and bra top side-seam edge. For the négligé, trim the same amount away from front and back side-seam edges.
For size 14, alter in the same places but add amounts.

To cut out
No seam allowance is included on the pattern. When cutting out add 1.5cm (⅝in) to all edges. Pin pattern pieces to fabric following the cutting layouts and cut out.
For the négligé belt cut 2 pieces of fabric 12cm × 95cm (4¾in × 37½in).
Transfer all pattern markings.

To make nightdress
1   With right sides together, tack and stitch darts in bra top, and press them towards the side.
2   Pin straight edge of lace to seam-line around bra top, mitring at corners. *See diagram 1.* Make a small dart 6.5cm (2½in) from side edge. Tack and stitch in place using a small zigzag stitch along straight edge of lace. On the wrong side trim away excess fabric. *See diagram 2.*
3   With right sides together, tack and stitch bra top to nightdress front. Press seam downward. Work a second row of stitching 6mm (¼in) away from the first. Trim seam allowance close to

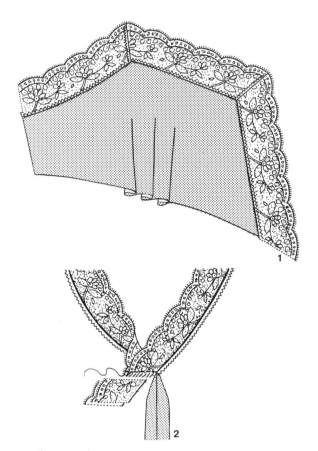

stitching and overcast raw edges. Press seam down.
4   On right side, top stitch close to the edge just below lace at centre front to hold seam in place.
5   Neaten raw edges of front and back seam edges.
6   Turn under seam allowance along back top, and tack close to folded edge. Trim to 1cm (⅜in). Neaten raw edge. On the right side, top stitch 6mm (¼in) from folded edge.
7   With right sides together, tack and stitch front to back at the side seams, leaving open below notch for slit. Press seam open.
Sew the seam allowance of slit to the garment by hand.
8   Neaten raw edge of hem and turn up. Stitch by hand or machine.
9   Sew ribbon straps to wrong side of top mitre on lace of bra top and to notch on nightdress back.
10   Cut 2 pieces of ribbon 20cm (8in) long. Sew one to top edge of lace at either side of centre front. Tie into a bow.

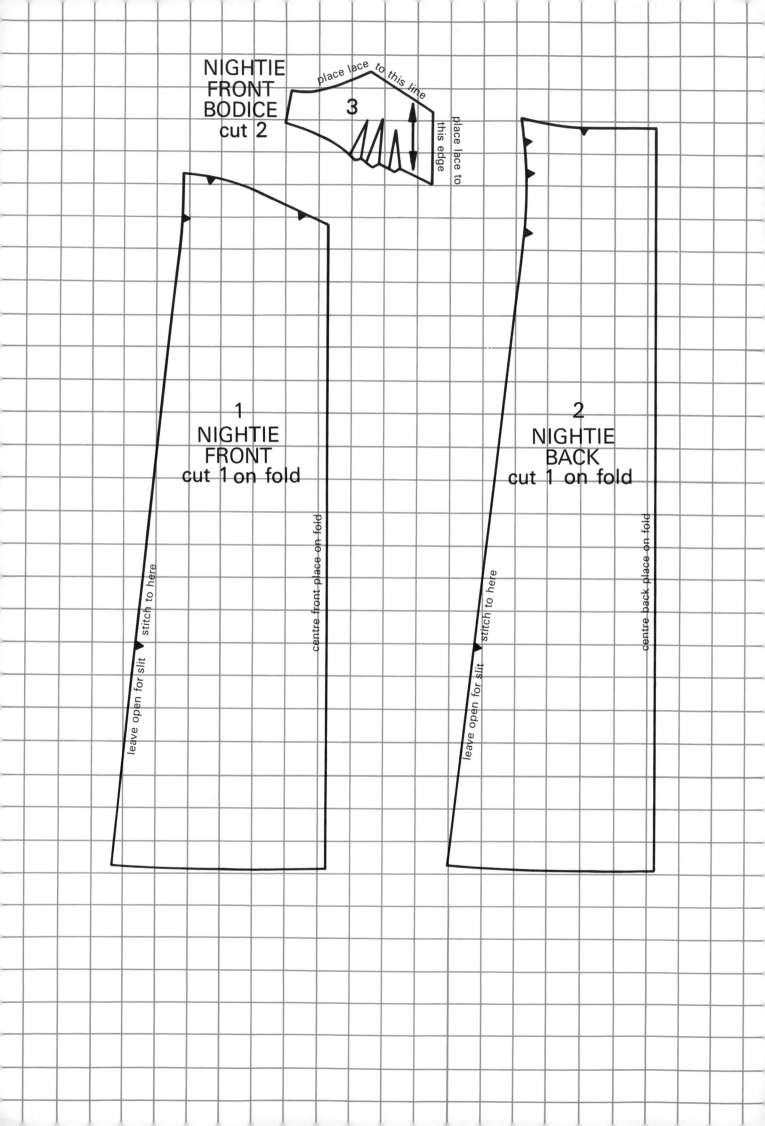

NIGHTIE
FRONT
BODICE
cut 2

3

place lace to this line

place lace to this edge

1
NIGHTIE
FRONT
cut 1 on fold

centre front place on fold

leave open for slit   stitch to here

2
NIGHTIE
BACK
cut 1 on fold

centre back place on fold

leave open for slit   stitch to here

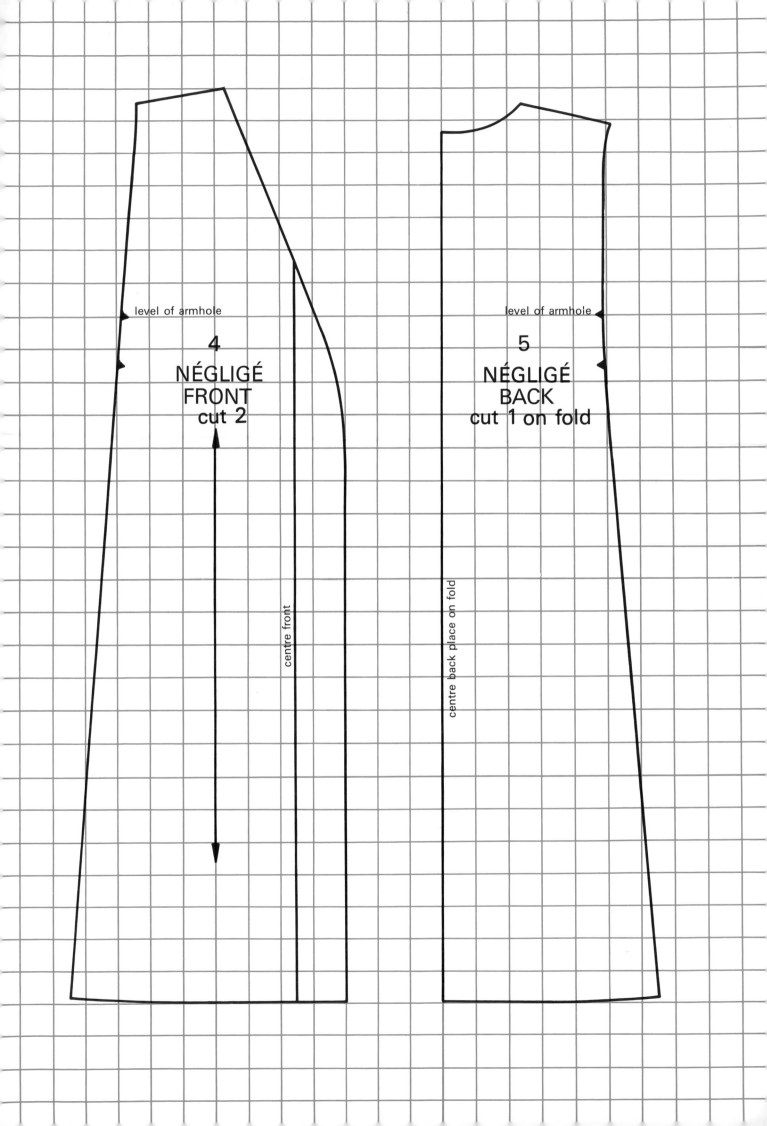

level of armhole

4

NÉGLIGÉ
FRONT
cut 2

centre front

level of armhole

5

NÉGLIGÉ
BACK
cut 1 on fold

centre back place on fold

To make négligé

1 Neaten raw edges of shoulder and side seams.

2 With right sides together, tack and stitch the fronts to the back at shoulder seams.

3 Lay the garment flat on the table, right side uppermost, and pin straight edge of lace to seamline down fronts and around back neck in one continuous strip, easing slightly over front curve. Tack in place.

Make 2 tiny darts in the lace each side of back neck to shape (*see page 132*).

Stitch lace in place with a fine zigzag stitch on the straight edge of the lace.

On the wrong side, trim excess fabric close to stitching (*see page 132*).

4 Apply lace in the same way to each armhole edge.

5 With right sides together, tack and stitch fronts to back at side seams. Press seams open. Press lace underarm seam towards back and zigzag stitch close to seamline. Trim away excess lace.

6 Neaten hem edge and turn up. Stitch by hand or machine.

7 With right sides together, tack and stitch two short ends of belt together. Press seam open. With right sides together, fold belt in half lengthwise. Tack and stitch long seam. Press seam open.

Turn belt to right side and press again so that the seam lies along centre of the belt. Shape ends diagonally, turn in raw edges and slipstitch to close.

8 Make belt carriers at side seams. Secure sewing thread 4cm (1½in) below waistline and, using a crochet hook, work a 7.5cm (3in) chain. Secure 4cm (1½in) above waistline.

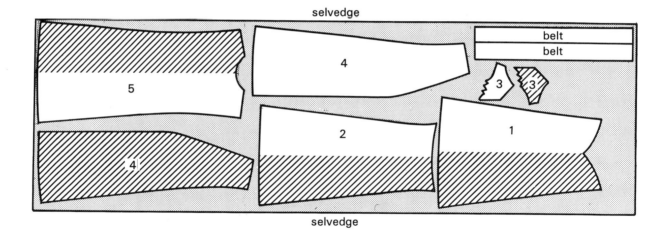

selvedge

selvedge

Silk pyjamas

Pamper yourself in pure silk crêpe-de-chine, the perfect fabric for luxury sleepwear. The pyjamas are made in a simple, classic style, and are very flattering.

Materials

4.8m (5¼yd) of 90cm (36in) wide fabric
70cm (¾yd) of 90cm (36in) wide interfacing (use organza or self fabric if making the pyjamas in silk)
4 buttons 1.3cm (½in)
2cm (¾in) wide elastic for trousers
sewing thread to match fabric
squared paper for pattern

Measurements

The pattern is given in size 12, for measurements see chart on page 123.

To make pattern

Draw up the pattern to scale from the graph pattern given here. One square represents 5cm (2in).

To adapt pattern

For size 10, cut away 1.3cm (½in) from jacket front and back side edges and sleeve underarm edges. Pleat out 2.5cm (1in) on trouser sides. For size 14, alter in the same places but add amounts.

To cut out

No seam allowance is included on the pattern. When cutting out add 1.5cm (⅝in) to all seam edges and hems, but add 4.2cm (1⅝in) to sleeve-hem and trouser-waist edges.
Pin pattern pieces to fabric following the cutting layout and cut out.
Transfer all pattern markings.

To make jacket

1   With right sides together, tack yoke to jacket back. Place right side of yoke facing to wrong side of jacket, tack and stitch through all thicknesses. Turn under seam allowance at yoke facing front edges and tack. Press yoke away from jacket. *See diagram 1.*
2   Tack interfacing to wrong side of front facings and collar facing.
Neaten the facing inner raw edge by working a row of machine stitching 6mm (¼in) from the edge, then overcast by hand or machine. Press flat.
3   With right sides together, fold the facing on the fold line. Tack and stitch from fold edge to

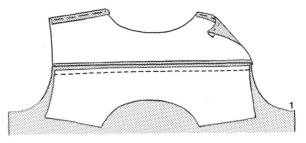

collar notch. Snip seam allowance almost to stitching at notch. *See diagram 2.*

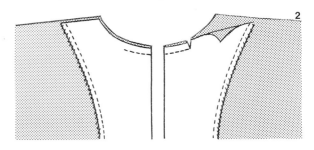

4   Turn to right side and tack front fold edges and neck edge close to seam edge. Tack facing to remainder of neck edge. Press flat. With right sides together, tack and stitch the jacket fronts to the yoke front. Press seams into yoke. *See diagram 3.*

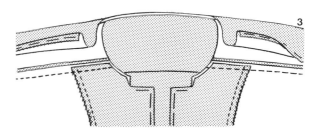

5   On wrong side, slipstitch the yoke-facing edges to the front-yoke seam stitching. Press flat. On right side, top stitch close to the yoke seams and then the width of the machine foot away.
6   With right sides together, tack and stitch the collar to the collar facing. Trim the interfacing close to the stitching and grade the seam allowance. Cut across corners and turn collar to right side. Tack close to stitched edge and press flat.
7   Matching centre backs and centre fronts, tack and stitch the interfaced edge of collar to neckline. Notch seam where necessary and press it towards collar.
On the inside, turn under the seam allowance on remaining edge of collar and slipstitch to stitching line. Press flat.

18

8   With right sides together, matching notches and circle to shoulder, tack and stitch sleeves into armholes. Press seam towards sleeve. Work a second row of stitching 6mm ($\frac{1}{4}$in) away from the first. Trim seam allowance close to the stitching and overcast the raw edge by hand or machine. On the right side, top stitch close to seam edge.

9   With right sides together, matching armhole seams, tack and stitch side and underarm seams in one operation. Neaten raw edges by hand or machine overcasting. Press seams open.

10   At the jacket-hem edge, open out the front facing, turn up 6mm ($\frac{1}{4}$in) and then a further 1.3cm ($\frac{1}{2}$in) and machine or hand stitch the hem. Press flat. Fold back the front facing and slipstitch to hem edge. Press flat.

11   At the sleeve-hem edges, turn up 1cm ($\frac{3}{8}$in) and then a further 3.2cm ($1\frac{1}{4}$in) and machine or hand stitch the hem. Press hem flat.

12   Make buttonholes on right front in positions indicated on pattern and sew buttons to left front to correspond.

To make trousers

1   With right sides together, tack and stitch the inside-leg seams. Work a second row of stitching 6mm ($\frac{1}{4}$in) away from the first.
Trim seam allowance close to the stitching and overcast the raw edge by hand or machine.

2   With right sides together, matching inside-leg seams, tack and stitch the crotch seam. Neaten seam raw edges as above.

3   At the trouser-top edge, turn over 1cm ($\frac{3}{8}$in) and then a further 3.2cm ($1\frac{1}{4}$in). Machine this casing, leaving an opening for inserting elastic. Cut a piece of elastic to fit the waist comfortably plus 1.3cm ($\frac{1}{2}$in) overlap. Insert elastic in waist casing, overlap ends and sew them securely together. Slipstitch opening in casing to close.

4   At trouser-hem edges, turn up 6mm ($\frac{1}{4}$in) then a further 1cm ($\frac{3}{8}$in) and sew hem by hand or machine. Press hem flat.

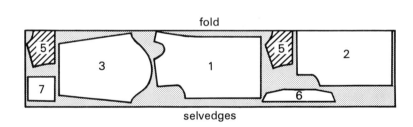

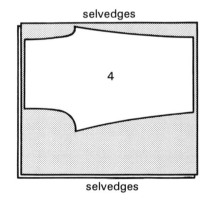

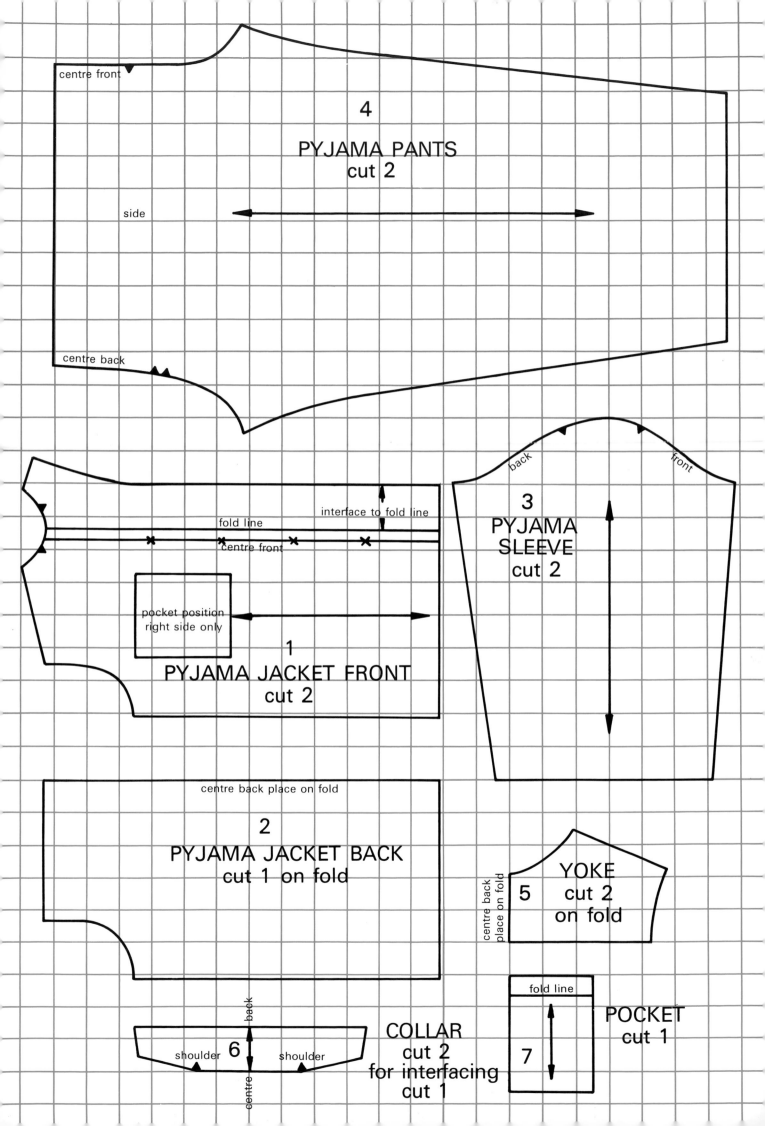

centre front

4

PYJAMA PANTS
cut 2

side

centre back

back   front

3
PYJAMA
SLEEVE
cut 2

interface to fold line

fold line

centre front

pocket position
right side only

1

PYJAMA JACKET FRONT
cut 2

centre back place on fold

2

PYJAMA JACKET BACK
cut 1 on fold

centre back
place on fold

5   **YOKE**
cut 2
on fold

fold line

POCKET
cut 1

7

back

shoulder   **6**   shoulder

centre

COLLAR
cut 2
for interfacing
cut 1

Winter nightdress

You won't feel the cold wearing this nightdress. Made in warm winceyette with a pretty yoke, high frilled collar and wrist-hugging sleeves, it is especially designed to keep the chills of winter away.

Materials
4.5m (5yd) of 115cm (45in) wide fabric
6mm ($\frac{1}{4}$in) wide elastic for wrists
sewing thread to match fabric
squared paper for pattern

Measurements
The pattern is given in size 12, for measurements see chart on page 123.

To make pattern
Draw up the pattern to scale from the graph pattern given here. One square represents 5cm (2in).

To adapt pattern
For size 10, cut away 1.3cm ($\frac{1}{2}$in) from front and back side edges and sleeve underarm edges. For size 14, alter in the same places but add amounts.

To cut out
No seam allowance is included on the pattern. When cutting out add 1.5cm ($\frac{5}{8}$in) to all seam edges and 2cm ($\frac{3}{4}$in) to sleeve and lower-hem edges.
Pin pattern pieces to fabric following the cutting layout and cut out.
For front neck ties cut 2 strips of fabric on straight of grain measuring 48cm × 5.7cm (19in × 2$\frac{1}{4}$in).
For sleeve casing cut out 2 strips of fabric 2.2cm ($\frac{7}{8}$in) wide on the straight of grain: 47cm (18$\frac{1}{2}$in) long for size 10; 49.5cm (19$\frac{1}{2}$in) for size 12; 52cm (20$\frac{1}{2}$in) for size 14.
Transfer all pattern markings.

To make nightdress
1   With right sides together, tack and stitch front yokes to back yoke at shoulder seams. Repeat for yoke facing. Press seams open.
2   Neaten top and short edges of collar by turning a narrow double hem and machine stitching. Press flat.
Work two rows of gathering stitches along seamline of lower edge of frill.
3   With right sides together, matching centre backs and having front-frill edges placed 1.5cm ($\frac{5}{8}$in) in from centre-front edge, pin frill to yoke

neck edge. Distribute the gathers evenly and tack in place.
4   Make neck ties by folding right sides together; stitch 1cm ($\frac{3}{8}$in) in from folded edge and across one end. Trim seam allowance to 6mm ($\frac{1}{4}$in) and turn ties to right side. Press flat.
5   Tack ties to yoke centre-front edges just below neck seamline. *See diagram 1.* With right sides together, tack and stitch yoke facing to yoke at the neck and centre-front edges, being careful not to catch the frill or the ties in the stitching. Trim the seam allowance, cut across corners and notch seam allowance at neck edge. *See diagram 2.* Turn to right side and tack close to front and neck edges. Press flat. *See diagram 3.*

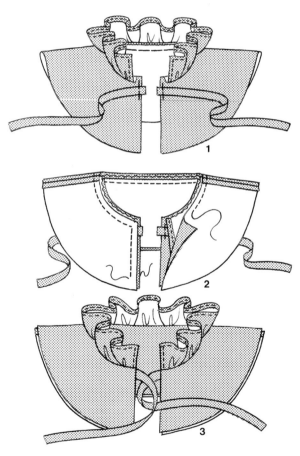

6   With right sides together, tack and stitch the sleeves to nightdress front and back. Work a second row of stitching the width of the machine foot away from the first. Trim seam allowance close to second row of stitching and neaten the raw edge by hand or machine overcasting. Press the seams towards the sleeves.
7   Reinforce the seamline at the nightdress centre front with small machine stitches. Snip seam allowance at centre front almost to

reinforcing stitches. Commencing and ending at the centre front, work two rows of gathering stitches around the entire top of the nightdress. *See diagram 4.*

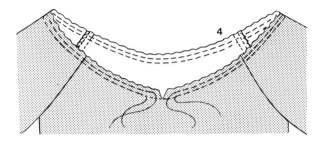

8 With right sides together, matching centre fronts, centre backs, and circles to shoulder seams, pin the nightdress to the yoke. Pull up the gathering threads and distribute the gathers evenly. Tack and stitch. Press the seam into the yoke. *See diagram 5.*

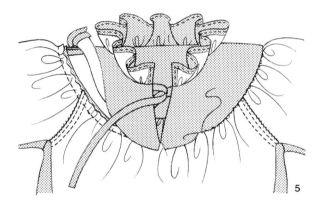

9 On wrong side, turn under the seam allowance on yoke-facing edge and slipstitch this to the line of stitching.
On right side of the yoke, work a row of top stitching close to the seam edge. Press yoke flat.
10 With right sides together, tack and stitch each sleeve underarm and garment side seam in one continuous seam. Work a second row of stitching the width of the machine foot away from the first. Trim the seam allowance close to the second row of stitching and neaten the raw edge by hand or machine overcasting. Press the seams towards the back.
11 At sleeve and lower-hem edges, turn under 6mm ($\frac{1}{4}$in) and then a further 1.3cm ($\frac{1}{2}$in). Machine and press flat.
12 With right sides together, join each sleeve casing to form a circle. Press seams open. Turn under 6mm ($\frac{1}{4}$in) on raw edges and tack.
With wrong sides together, matching seam to underarm seam, tack and stitch casing to position indicated on pattern, leaving a small opening for inserting elastic.
13 Cut 2 pieces of elastic, each to fit the wrist comfortably plus 6mm ($\frac{1}{4}$in) overlap. Insert elastic into sleeve casings, overlap ends and sew securely together. Slipstitch opening to close.

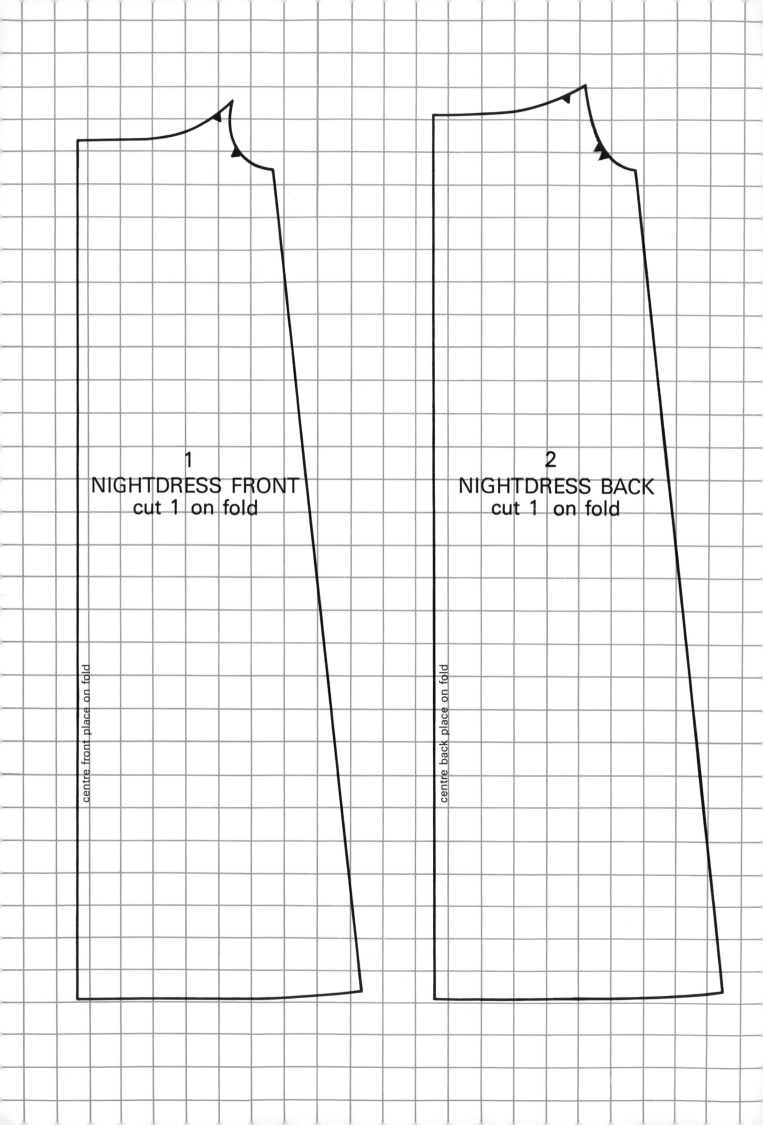

1
NIGHTDRESS FRONT
cut 1 on fold

centre front place on fold

2
NIGHTDRESS BACK
cut 1 on fold

centre back place on fold

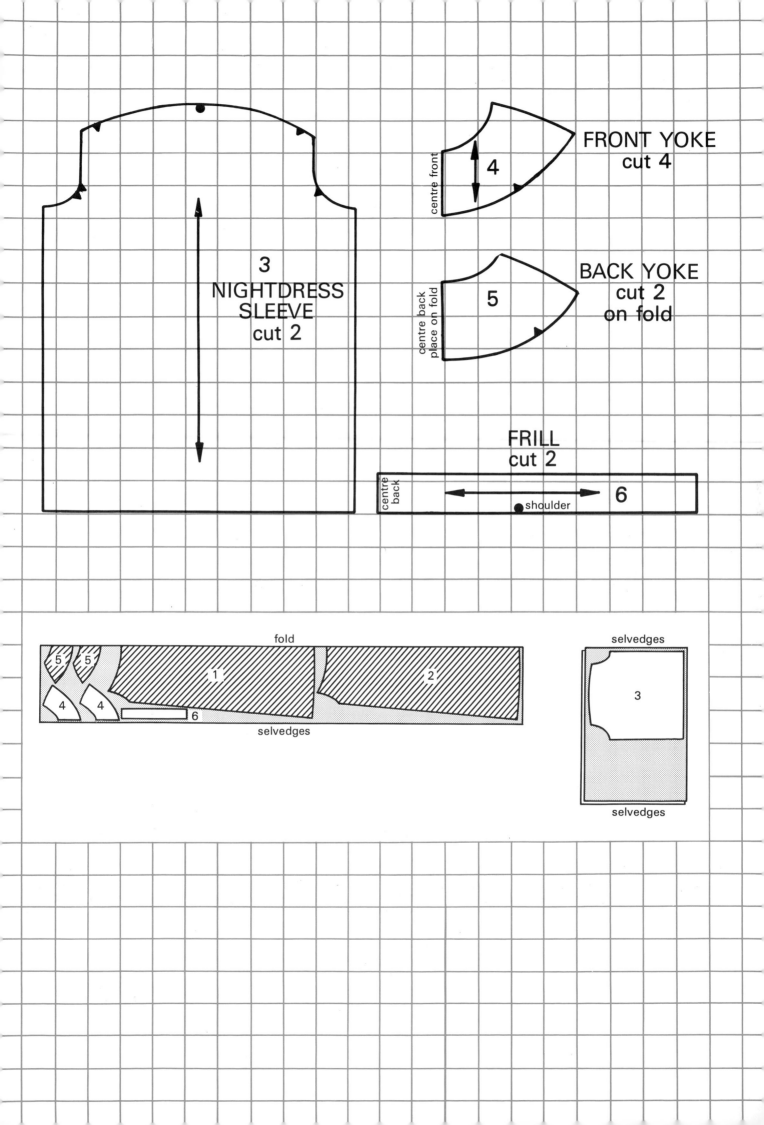

3
NIGHTDRESS
SLEEVE
cut 2

FRONT YOKE
cut 4

4

centre front

BACK YOKE
cut 2
on fold

5

centre back
place on fold

FRILL
cut 2

centre back

6

shoulder

fold

5   5

4   4

1

2

6

selvedges

selvedges

3

selvedges

Quilted bedjacket

Quick and simple to make, this lovely bedjacket is delicately quilted with appliquéd lace flower motifs. The motifs are simply machine stitched in place with a zigzag stitch.

Materials
2.8m (3⅓yd) of 90cm (36in) wide polyester/cotton fabric
2.8m (3⅓yd) of 90cm (36in) wide polyester lining fabric
2.8m (3⅓yd) of 100cm (39in) wide medium weight polyester wadding
50cm (½yd) of 90cm wide patterned net with large flowers
3.7m (4yd) of white bias binding
tiny pink pearl beads
pink irridescent sequins
sewing thread to match fabric and net
squared paper for pattern

Measurements
The pattern is given in size 12, for measurements see chart on page 123.

To make pattern
Draw up the pattern to scale from the graph pattern given here. One square represents 5cm (2in).

To adapt pattern
For size 10, cut away 1.3cm (½in) from front and back side seams and sleeve underarm seams. For size 14, alter in the same places but add amounts.

To cut out
No seam allowance is included on the pattern. When cutting out add 4cm (1½in) to all edges of pattern pieces 1, 2 and 3 to allow for shrinkage in quilting and 1.5cm (⅝in) to all other edges. Pin pattern pieces to fabric following the cutting layouts and cut out. Transfer all pattern markings.

To make the bedjacket
1 Using diagonal stitches, baste the lining, wadding and top fabric pieces together with right sides uppermost. Work from the centre outwards and place the rows 10cm (4in) apart.
2 Cut out flowers from the net and pin them at random on the garment pieces, making sure that the arrangements match on fronts, backs and sleeves. Machine the flowers in place with a small zigzag stitch.

3 Pin the paper patterns onto the quilted pieces and trim away the excess fabric, leaving a seam allowance of 1.5cm (⅝in) on all edges. Tack close to all edges through all thicknesses.
4 With right sides together, stitch the centre-back seam.
5 Stay stitch round front and back neck edges.
6 With right sides together, join fronts to back at shoulder and side seams.
Neaten the seam edges by trimming away 6mm (¼in) of wadding and lining from the seam allowance. *See diagram 1.* Turn under 6mm (¼in) on seam edges and hem to lining. *See diagram 2.*

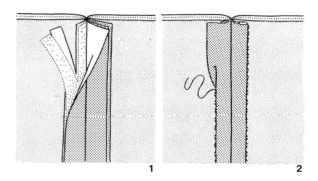

7 Work two rows of gathering stitches between the notches on the sleeve head. With right sides together, stitch the underarm seam and neaten it as described above.
8 With right sides together, matching underarm seams and notches, pin the sleeve into the armhole, easing in fullness at sleeve head to fit evenly. Stitch the seam with the sleeve uppermost. *See diagram 3.* Work a second row of stitching 6mm (¼in) away from the first. Trim seam allowance close to stitching and neaten raw edge by hand or machine overcasting. *See diagram 4.*

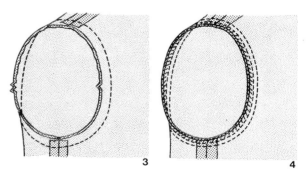

9 With right sides together, tack and stitch bias binding to hem edge. Turn up bias binding plus 6mm (¼in) hem and slipstitch to inside. Press flat.

10 With right sides together, tack and stitch bias binding to jacket fronts. Fold binding over raw edge and slipstitch folded edge to line of stitching.

Fold edges back along fold line and tack close to folded edge. Press flat. Slipstitch the bound edge to the lining. Slipstitch edges together at hem.

11 Using the width of the presser-foot as a guide, top stitch the centre-front and hem edges.

12 Finish hems on sleeve edges in the same way.

13 With right sides together, fold the neck ties in half lengthwise and stitch the long edges, leaving short ends open. Turn to right side. Press the seam to the centre back of the tie. Turn in raw edges at one end and slipstitch them together.

14 With right sides together, matching centre backs, tack and stitch the neck trim to the neck edge.

Clip curves. Cut off excess fabric at centre fronts of neck trim to 1.5cm ($\frac{5}{8}$in). Turn back the seam allowance at centre fronts of neck-trim and tack. Machine the neck ties to centre fronts of neck-trim.

Turn 1.3cm ($\frac{1}{2}$in) along raw edge of neck-trim to wrong side and slipstitch the folded edge to stitching line on wrong side of jacket.

15 Sew beads and sequins in centre of each flower and at the join of the neck ties.

FABRIC and LINING

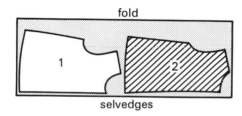 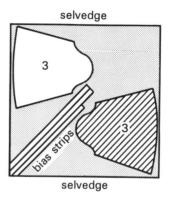

WADDING

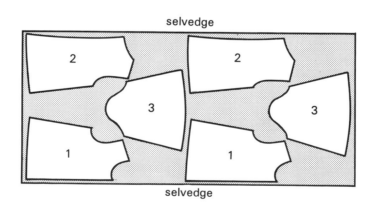

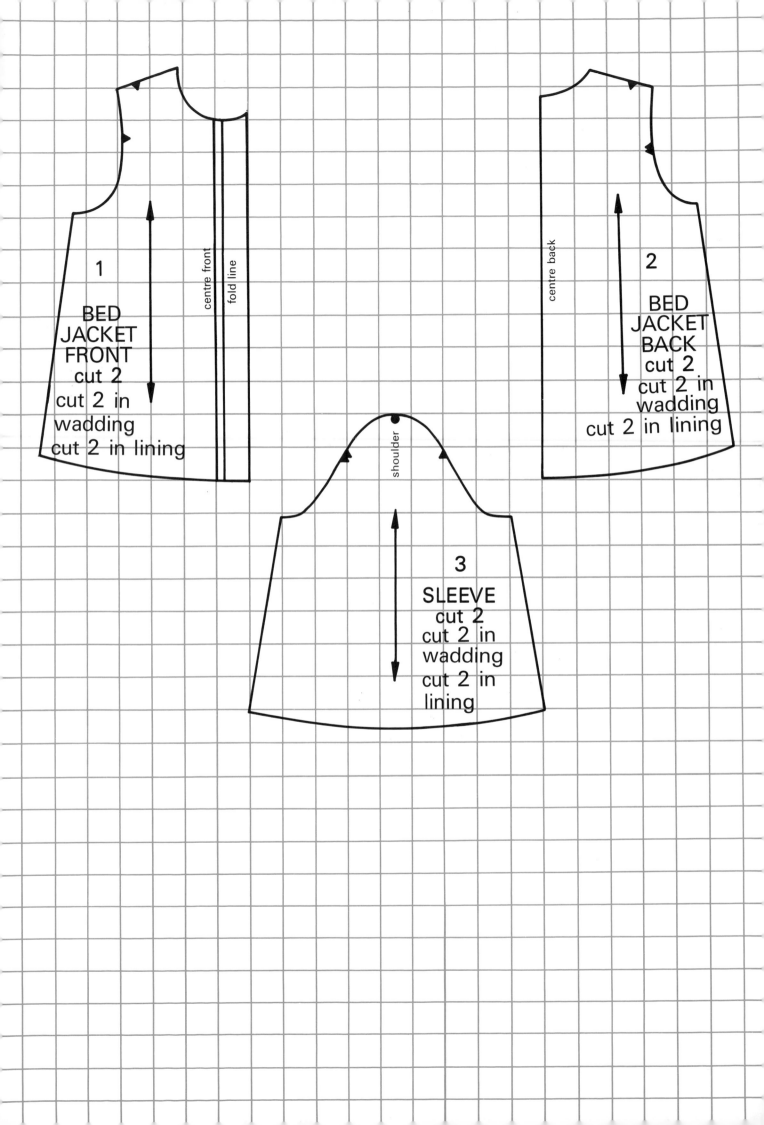

1

BED
JACKET
FRONT
cut 2
cut 2 in
wadding
cut 2 in lining

centre front

fold line

2

BED
JACKET
BACK
cut 2
cut 2 in
wadding
cut 2 in lining

centre back

shoulder

3

SLEEVE
cut 2
cut 2 in
wadding
cut 2 in
lining

Sleepsuit & jacket

A delightful twosome in the lightest polyester crêpe-de-chine. The bra top to the sleepsuit is prettily trimmed with deep lace. The little jacket simply ties at the neckline.

Materials
3.5m (3¾yd) of 115cm (45in) wide polyester crêpe-de-chine
2.6m (2⅞yd) of 5.5cm (2¼in) wide nylon lace trimming
7 buttons 1cm (⅜in)
sewing thread to match lace
sewing thread to match fabric
squared paper for patterns

Measurements
The pattern is given in size 12, for measurements see chart on page 123.

To make pattern
Draw up the pattern to scale from the graph pattern given here. One square represents 5cm (2in).

To adapt pattern
For size 10, cut away 1.3cm (½in) from jacket front and back side edges, and front and back side edges of sleepsuit pants. Cut away 1.3cm (½in) from sleepsuit-top back side edge and 6mm (¼in) from top edges of bra top.
For size 14, alter in the same places but add amounts.

To cut out
No seam allowance is included on the pattern. When cutting out add 1.5cm (⅝in) to all edges. Pin pattern pieces to fabric following the cutting layouts and cut out.
Transfer all pattern markings.

To make jacket
1   With right sides together, tack and stitch shoulder and side seams.
Press seams open. Notch side seam where necessary. Neaten raw edges by hand or machine overcasting.
2   At armhole and lower-hem edges turn under 6mm (¼in) and then a further 1cm (⅜in); slipstitch hem in place.
3   Cut 2 pieces of lace for front edges, matching up pattern, and allow for a narrow hem on lower edge of each. Turn in and machine this narrow hem.
Tack lace to right side of jacket on seamline.

Machine stitch in place, then work a fine zigzag stitch over first line of stitching.
On wrong side, trim back excess seam allowance close to stitching.
4   For neck binding and ties, cut 2 bias strips of fabric measuring 50cm × 3.5cm (20in × 1⅜in). Join to make one strip.
Trim seam allowance away from neckline. Stay stitch close to neck raw edge. With right sides together, tack and stitch bias strip to neck edge, having the join at centre back and taking a 6mm (¼in) seam. Press seam upwards. *See diagram 1.*

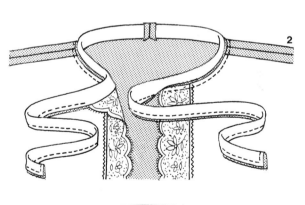

5   With right sides together, tack and stitch the loose ends. *See diagram 2.* Turn rouleaux to right side.
Turn under seam allowance at neck edge and slipstitch to stitching line. *See diagram 3.*

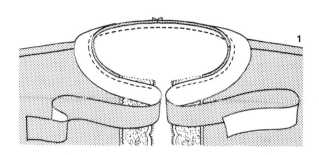

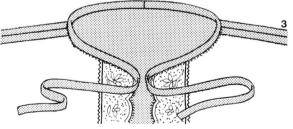

To make sleepsuit

1   With right sides together, matching notches, tack and stitch side seams and inside-leg seams. Press seams open. Neaten raw edges by hand or machine overcasting.

2   With right sides together, fold back the facings at front opening. Tack and stitch 1cm ($\frac{3}{8}$in) in on top edges and stitch bottom edges diagonally to dot. Trim seam allowances and snip seam allowance to dot. Turn to right side and tack close to all edges. Press flat. *See diagram 4.*

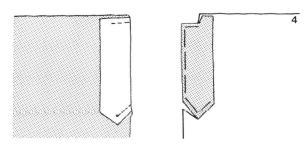

3   Stitch facings at leg lower edges in the same way as the front-opening facings.

4   With right sides together, matching notches and inside-leg seams, tack and stitch the crotch seam from the lower edge of the front facing to the centre back. *See diagram 5.* Neaten seam edges by hand or machine overcasting. Press seam open and notch on curve where necessary.

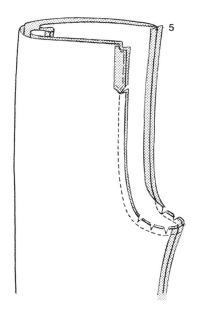

5   Work 2 rows of gathering stitches at leg edges and between notches at top edges.
6   Draw up gathers to make entire leg edge measure 28cm (11in).

For each leg, cut a strip of lace measuring 28cm (11in) and turn in a very narrow hem on each raw edge.
Pin and tack lace to leg-edge seamline, distributing the gathers evenly. Stitch in place with a line of straight stitching and then fine zigzag stitches.
On wrong side, trim the excess seam allowance close to the stitching.

7   For the shoulder-straps, cut 2 bias strips of fabric measuring 50cm × 3.5cm ($19\frac{3}{4}$in × $1\frac{3}{8}$in). Make two rouleau straps, stitching 6mm ($\frac{1}{4}$in) from folded edge.

8   Tack straps to right side of back yoke in positions indicated on the pattern.
With right sides together, tack and stitch the back-yoke facing to the back yoke along top edge only. Turn to right side and tack close to stitched edge, rolling seam slightly to the wrong side. Press flat.

9   With wrong sides together, tack bra sections to bra facings.
Using template as a guide, shape lace with tucks to fit round bra sections, matching pattern at centre front.
Stitch tucks; zigzag stitch close to stitching line and trim off excess lace.
Sew lace to bra-section edges as instructed above.

10   With right sides together, tack and stitch the bra-side lace to back yoke.

11   With right sides together, matching notches and side seams, and distributing the gathers evenly, tack and stitch the bra and back yoke to the sleepsuit pants top. Work a second row of stitching 6mm ($\frac{1}{4}$in) away from the first, trim seam allowance close to stitching and neaten raw edge by hand or machine overcasting. Press seam upwards.

12   Turn under the seam allowance on back-yoke facing and tack. On the wrong side slipstitch to yoke stitching line at side and lower edges. Press flat.

13   Adjust shoulder straps to fit and sew in place commencing at top of fabric bra section onto back of lace.

14   Work 3 buttonholes on front right edge and 2 buttonholes on each ankle front opening edge, 1 placed 6mm ($\frac{1}{4}$in) up from lace edging and the second 2.5cm (1in) above. Sew buttons on front left edge of jacket and back edges of ankle openings to correspond.

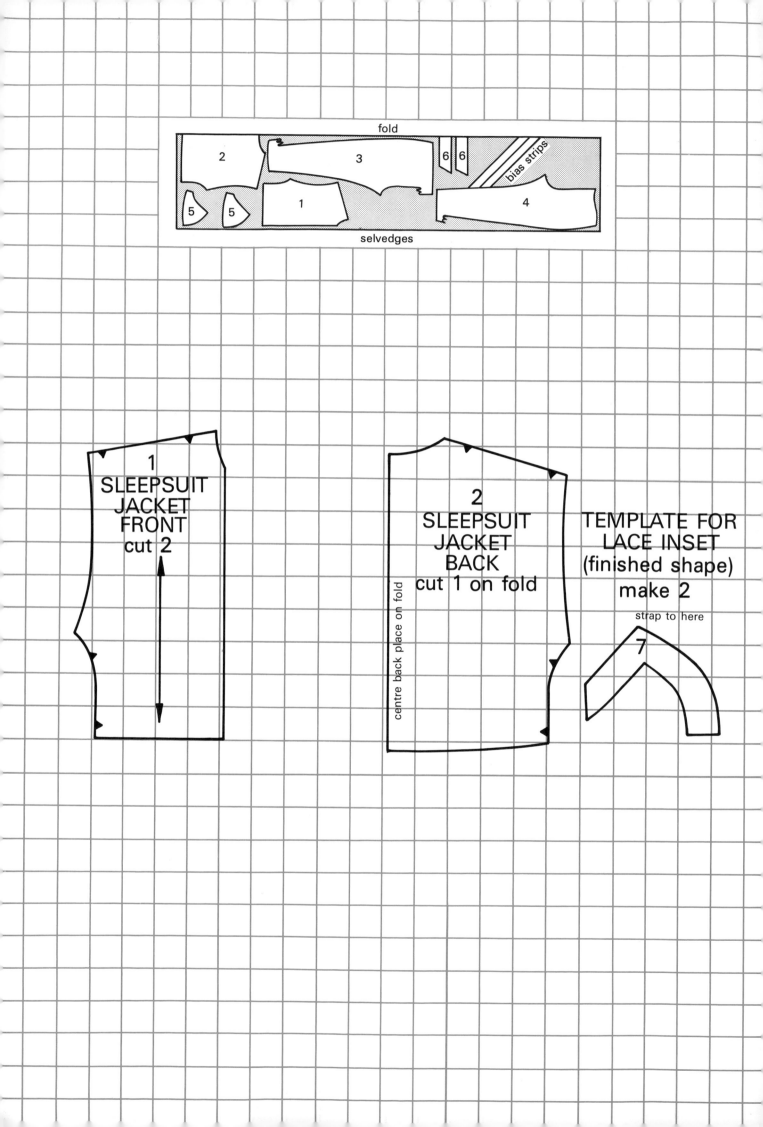

fold

2

3

6 6

bias strips

5 5

1

4

selvedges

1
SLEEPSUIT
JACKET
FRONT
cut 2

2
SLEEPSUIT
JACKET
BACK
cut 1 on fold

centre back place on fold

TEMPLATE FOR
LACE INSET
(finished shape)
make 2

strap to here

7

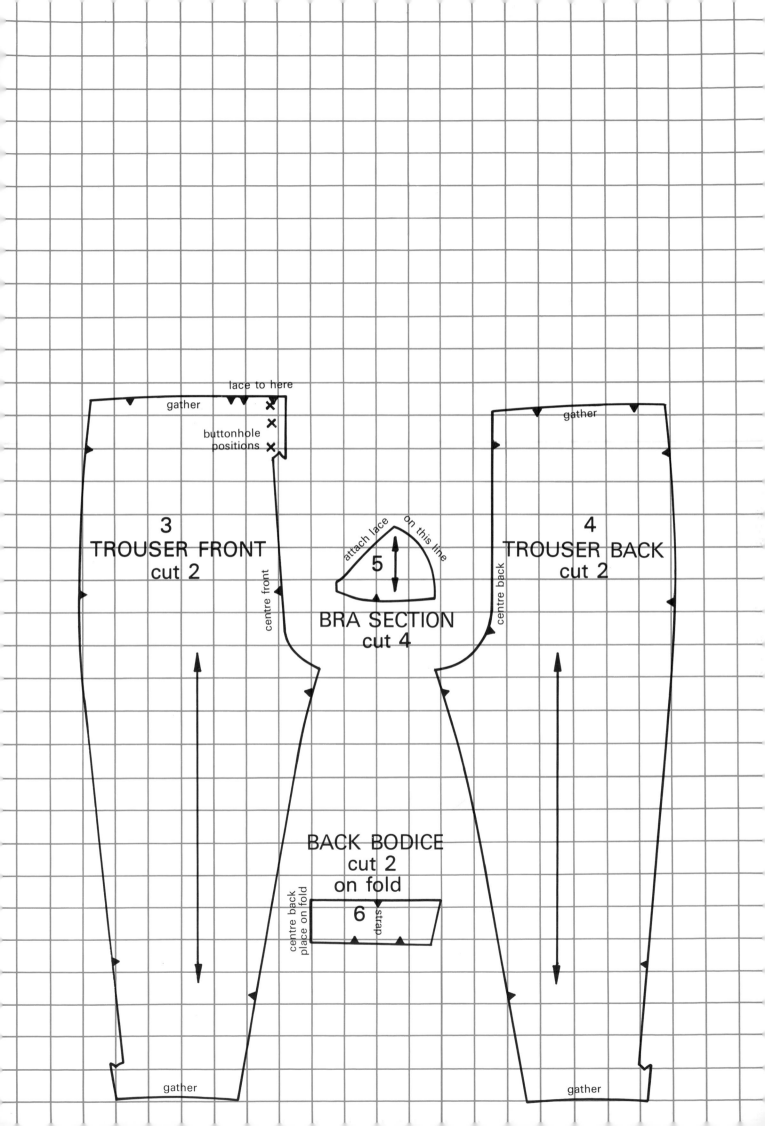

lace to here

gather

3
TROUSER FRONT
cut 2

buttonhole
positions

centre front

attach lace

on this line

5

BRA SECTION
cut 4

gather

4
TROUSER BACK
cut 2

centre back

BACK BODICE
cut 2
on fold

centre back
place on fold

6

strap

gather

gather

Knitted vest & knickers

Knitted in mercerised cotton, this vest and knickers set is decorated with simple embroidered flowers. These garments could also be worn as shorts and top for the beach.

Materials

Vest: 5[5:6] 50g balls Pingouin Fil d'Ecosse No 5 in main colour (A); 1 ball in each of two contrasting colours (B) and (C); an oddment in 3rd contrasting colour (D) for centre of embroidered flowers.

Knickers: 4[4:5] 50g balls of Pingouin Fil d'Ecosse No 5 in main colour (A); 1 ball in 2nd contrasting colour (C); an oddment in 3rd contrasting colour (D) for centre of embroidered flowers.

1 pair each of $2\frac{1}{4}$mm (No 13) and 3mm (No 11) knitting needles; a large-eyed embroidery needle; a waist length of 2.5cm (1in) wide elastic for knickers.

Measurements

Vest: To fit bust 83 [87:92]cm (32[34:36]in); length: 60[61:62]cm ($23\frac{1}{2}$[24:$24\frac{1}{2}$]in).

Knickers: To fit hips 87[92:97]cm (34[36:38]in); length: 33.5[34.5:36.5]cm ($13\frac{1}{4}$[$13\frac{3}{4}$:$14\frac{1}{4}$]in).

Note: Follow instructions in [ ] for larger sizes.

Tension: 15 sts to 5cm (2in).

Abbreviations

K = knit; p = purl; st(s) = stitch(es); st st = stocking stitch; inc = increase; dec = decrease; tog = together; mm = millimetres; cm = centimetres; in = inch(es).

Vest

FRONT: With $2\frac{1}{4}$mm (No 13) needles and A, cast on 94[100:108] sts.

Work in k1, p1 rib for 2cm ($\frac{3}{4}$in).

Inc row: Rib 3[6:10], (inc in next st, rib 2) repeat ( ) to last 1[4:8] sts, rib to end (124[130:138] sts).

Change to 3mm (No 11) needles.

Proceed in st st working in stripes of 18 rows A, 4 rows B until the 16th row of the 7th stripe in A has been worked.

To shape armhole: Continuing in stripes, cast off 4 sts at beg of next 2 rows. Dec 1 st each end of next and every following alternate row until 92[96:100] sts remain.

Work 7[9:11] rows straight, ending with p row.

To divide for neck: K27 [28:30], k2 tog, turn and leave remaining sts on a spare needle.

Work on first set of sts as follows: Dec 1 st at

neck edge on every row to 20[21:23] sts, then on every following alternate row until 11[12:14] sts remain.

Work straight until the 12th[16th:18th] row of the 11th stripe in A has been worked, ending with p row. *3rd size only*: Work 4 rows in B.

To shape shoulder (all sizes): Cast off 6 sts at beg of next row. Work 1 row. Cast off.

Return to sts on spare needle. With right side facing place next 34[36:36] sts on a holder, join yarn to next st, k2 tog, k to end of row.

Complete to match first side reversing shaping.

BACK: Work as given for front to completion of armhole shaping: 92[96:100] sts.

Work straight until the 4th[8th:14th] row of the 10th stripe in A has been worked, ending with p row.

To shape neck: K27[28:30], k2 tog, turn and leave remaining sts on a spare needle.

Work on first set of sts as follows: Dec 1 st at neck edge on every row until 11[12:14] sts remain.

Work 6 rows straight, ending with p row.

To shape shoulder: Cast off 6 sts at beg of next row. Work 1 row. Cast off.

Return to sts on spare needle.

With right side facing place next 34[36:36] sts on a holder, join yarn to next st, k2 tog, k to end of row.

Complete to match first side reversing shaping.

NECKBAND: Join right shoulder seam. With right side facing join C to shoulder at left front neck and using a $2\frac{1}{4}$mm (No 13) needle k up 50 sts from left front neck, k the sts from holder, k up 50 sts from right front neck, 22 sts from right back neck, k the sts from holder, then k up 22 sts from left back neck (212[216:216]sts).

Work in k1, p1 rib for 2cm ($\frac{3}{4}$in).

Cast off in rib.

Join left shoulder and neckband seam.

ARMHOLE BORDERS (*both alike*): With right side facing join on C and using a $2\frac{1}{4}$mm (No 13) needle k up 152[160:168] sts evenly all round armhole. Work in k1, p1 rib for 2cm ($\frac{3}{4}$in).

Cast off in rib.

TO COMPLETE: See yarn label for pressing details. Following *diagram 1* for daisy stitch, work flowers in B and C on front as shown in photograph. Following *diagram 2* for bullion stitch, finish centre of each flower with D. Join side seams.

Knickers

LEFT BACK: With $2\frac{1}{4}$mm (No 13) needles and C,

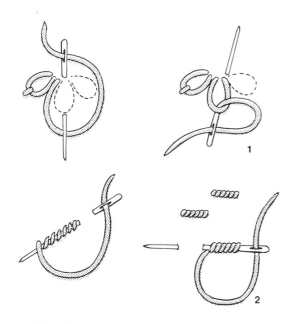

cast on 80[84:88] sts.

Work 9 rows k1, p1 rib increasing 1 st at beg of every alternate row (84[88:92] sts).

Cut off C. Join on A.

Change to 3mm (No 11) needles.

Proceed in st st increasing 1 st at beg of next and every following alternate row to 91[95:99] sts.

Work 3 rows straight, ending with p row.

To shape crotch: Cast off 13 sts at beg of next row and 3 sts at beg of following 2 alternate rows.

Work 1 row. Dec 1 st at shaped edge on every row to 67[71:75] sts, then on every following 4th row until 63[67:71] sts remain. Work straight to

33.5[34.5:36.5]cm ($13\frac{1}{4}$[$13\frac{3}{4}$:$14\frac{1}{4}$]in) from cast-on edge, ending with k row.

Next row: K to form hemline. Beg with k row, work 10 rows st st. Cast off.

RIGHT BACK: As left back, reversing shaping.

LEFT FRONT: With $2\frac{1}{4}$mm (No 13) needles and C, cast on 66[70:74]sts.

Work 9 rows k1, p1 rib increasing 1 st at beg of 5th row (67[71:75] sts).

Cut off C. Join on A.

Change to 3mm (No 11) needles.

Proceed in st st increasing 1 st at end of next and every following 4th row to 71[75:79] sts.

Work 5 rows straight.

Dec 1 st at shaped edge on every row to 62[66:70] sts, then on every following alternate row to 57[61:65] sts. Work straight to 33.5[34.5:36.5]cm ($13\frac{1}{4}$[$13\frac{3}{4}$:$14\frac{1}{4}$]in) from cast-on edge, ending with k row.

Next row: K to form hemline.

Beg with k row, work 10 rows st st.

Cast off.

RIGHT FRONT: As left front, reversing shaping.

TO COMPLETE: See yarn label for pressing details.

Following *diagram 1* for daisy stitch, work flowers in B and C on right front as shown in photograph. Following *diagram 2* for bullion stitch, finish centre of each flower with D. Join centre front and back seams, then join crotch and inner leg seams. Fold hem to wrong side and slipstitch in position, leaving an opening. Insert elastic, then slipstitch the opening.

Floral pyjamas

Easy to care for polyester/cotton lawn has been used to make these pyjamas. Lightweight and crease resisting, they are ideal to take on holiday.

Materials
4m (4⅓yd) of 115cm (45in) wide polyester/cotton lawn
1m (1¼yd) of 3mm (⅛in) wide elastic
60cm (⅔yd) of 6mm (¼in) wide elastic
3 buttons 1.5cm (⅝in)
sewing thread to match fabric
squared paper for pattern

Measurements
The pattern is given in size 12, for measurements see chart on page 123.

To make pattern
Draw up the pattern to scale from the graph pattern given here. One square represents 5cm (2in).

To adapt pattern
For size 10, cut away 1.3cm (½in) from jacket front and back side edges, and pleat out 2.5cm (1in) on trouser sides.
For size 14, alter in the same places but add amounts.

To cut out
No seam allowance is included on the pattern. When cutting out add 1.5cm (⅝in) to all seam edges, 2cm (¾in) to trouser-top edge and 2.5cm (1in) to trouser-hem edge.
Pin pattern pieces to fabric following the cutting layout and cut out.
Transfer all pattern markings.

To make jacket
1 Work two rows of gathering stitches between notches on jacket fronts and back.
2 With right sides together, matching notches, pin jacket fronts and back to the yokes, pulling up the gathers to fit. Distribute the gathers evenly and stitch. Press seams towards yoke.
3 Reinforce the inner corners at circles on collar. Slash to circles. Tack and stitch centre-back seam of collar. Press seam open. *See diagram 1.*
Matching centre backs and notches, tack and stitch collar to neckline. Notch seam allowance. Press seam towards collar. *See diagrams 2 and 3.*
4 Reinforce the inner corners at circles on front and collar facings. Slash to circles. Neaten front-facing inner edges by hand or machine

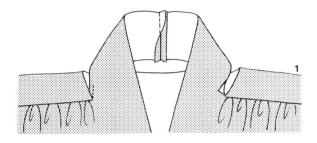

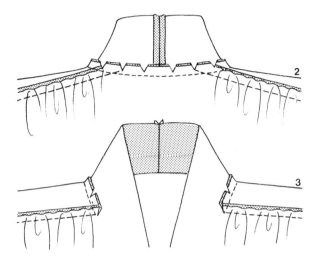

overcasting. With right sides together, tack and stitch centre-back seam. Press seam open.
5 With right sides together, matching centre-back seams, tack and stitch the front and collar facing to the jacket fronts and collar. Notch seam allowance on curves where necessary. Turn to right side and tack close to stitched edge. Press stitched edge flat.
6 Turn under seam allowance on yoke-facing long edges and tack. Trim seam allowance from shoulder edge of yoke facing.
Pin facing to wrong side of yoke having neck edges level, and slipstitch to machine stitching. Press flat.
7 Turn under seam allowance at neck and shoulder edges and slipstitch to machine stitching and yoke edge. Press flat. *See diagram 4.*

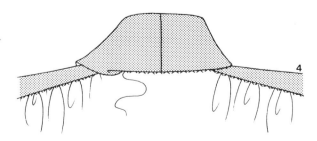

45

8 With right sides together, fold welt in half and stitch short ends. Trim seam allowance and turn to right side and tack close to stitched and top folded edges. Press flat.

With right sides together and with the raw edges towards the yoke, tack and stitch the welt to the left front as indicated on pattern. Trim seam allowance to 6mm ($\frac{1}{4}$in) and press welt upwards. Machine short ends to jacket.

9 With right sides together, tack and stitch side seams. Press seams open.

10 At hem and armhole edges, turn under 6mm ($\frac{1}{4}$in) and then a further 1cm ($\frac{3}{8}$in) and slipstitch in place. Fold front facings to wrong side and slipstitch to hem edge. Press hems flat.

11 For waist, cut 2 pieces of 3mm ($\frac{1}{8}$in) wide elastic measuring 40.5cm (16in) for size 10; 46cm (18in) for size 12; 51cm (20in) for size 14. Pin elastic at each end and at centre back in positions marked on pattern and stitch in place, stretching the elastic whilst doing so.

12 Make buttonholes on right front in positions indicated on pattern and sew buttons to left front to correspond.

To make trousers

1 With right sides together, tack and stitch the inside-leg seams. Press seams open and neaten raw edges by hand or machine overcasting.

2 With right sides together, matching inside-leg seams, tack and stitch the crotch seam. Press seam open and neaten raw edges.

3 At waist edge turn under 6mm ($\frac{1}{4}$in) and then a further 1.3cm ($\frac{1}{2}$in) and machine casing, leaving an opening at centre back. Cut a length of elastic to fit the waist comfortably plus 6mm ($\frac{1}{4}$in). Insert elastic in casing, overlap ends 6mm ($\frac{1}{4}$in) and stitch securely. Slipstitch opening in casing to close.

4 Try on trousers and adjust length. Trim seam allowance to 3.2cm ($1\frac{1}{4}$in). Turn under 6mm ($\frac{1}{4}$in) and then a further 2.5cm (1in) and slipstitch hem. Press hem flat.

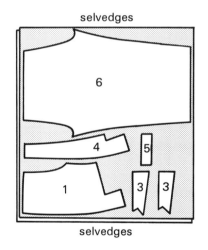

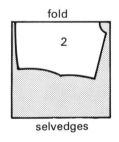

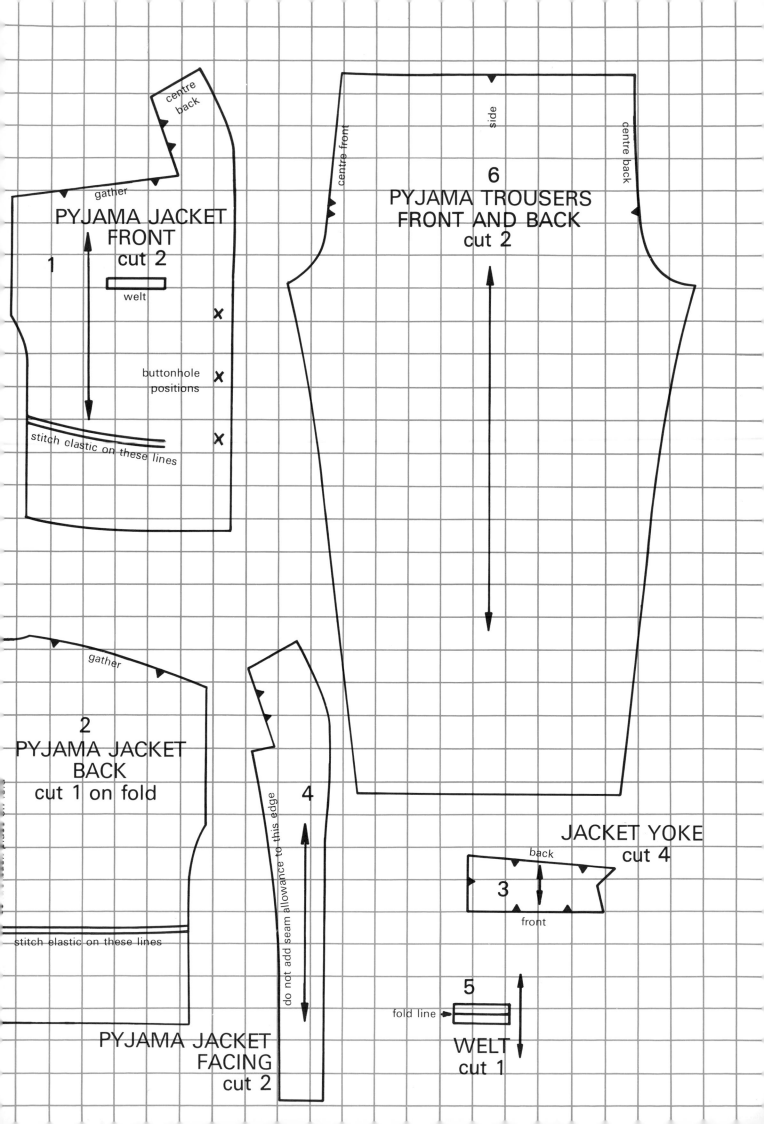

centre back

gather

PYJAMA JACKET
FRONT
cut 2

1

welt

✗

buttonhole
positions ✗

stitch elastic on these lines ✗

side

6

PYJAMA TROUSERS
FRONT AND BACK
cut 2

centre front

centre back

gather

2
PYJAMA JACKET
BACK
cut 1 on fold

4

do not add seam allowance to this edge

stitch elastic on these lines

PYJAMA JACKET
FACING
cut 2

JACKET YOKE
cut 4

back

3

front

5

fold line

WELT
cut 1

Towelling/Stretch terry sleepsuit

A super sleepsuit ideal for chilly nights. In this gay red and white stripe it looks too good to keep for bedtime only

Materials

4m (4½yd) of 90cm (36in) wide stretch towelling/stretch terry
2cm (¾in) wide elastic to fit waist plus 1.3cm (½in)
30cm (12in) of fine piping cord cut into 5cm (2in) pieces for buttonhole loops
6 ball buttons 1cm (⅜in)
sewing thread to match fabric
squared paper for pattern

Measurements

The pattern is given in size 12, for measurements see chart on page 123.

To make pattern

Draw up the pattern to scale from the graph pattern given. One square represents 5cm (2in).

To adapt pattern

For size 10, cut away 1.3cm (½in) from front and back side seams, and underarm seams of top.
Pleat out 2.5cm (1in) down the centre of pants pattern piece.
For size 14, alter in the same places but add amounts.

To cut out

No seam allowance is included on the pattern.
When cutting out add 1.5cm (⅝in) to all seam edges, 3cm (1¼in) to top and pants-hem edges, and 4cm (1½in) to pants-top edge.
Pin pattern pieces to fabric following the cutting layout and cut out.
Transfer all pattern markings.

To make top

1   Sew piping cord buttonhole loops on each back shoulder seam, the first placed 2.5cm (1in) in from armhole edge and a further two at 4cm (1½in) intervals.
2   Tack and stitch neck facings to front and back necklines and across shoulders in one line of stitching. Trim seam allowance and turn to right side. Tack close to edge. Press flat. Topstitch 1cm (⅜in) from edge. *See diagram 1.*
3   Tack and stitch front to back at side seams. Work a second row of stitching 6mm (¼in) away from the first. Trim seam allowance back to stitching and overcast raw edges by hand or machine.

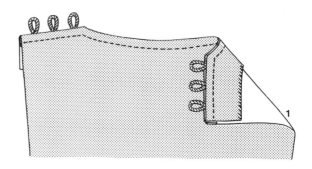

4   Tack and stitch sleeve underarm seam. Press seam open.
5   Having shoulder seams edge to edge, matching underarm seams, and with circle to shoulder point, tack and stitch sleeve into armhole. *See diagram 2.*
6   Turn under seam allowance on sleeve free edge and hem this to the armhole seam. *See diagram 3.*

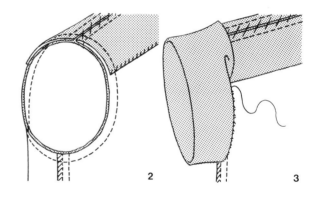

7   Turn up hem 1cm (⅜in) and tack. Turn up a further 2cm (¾in) and machine.
8   Sew buttons 1cm (⅜in) in from front shoulder edge to correspond with button loops.

To make pants

1 With right sides together tack and stitch inside-leg seams.

2 Turn one leg to the right side and slip it inside the other.
Matching inside leg seams, tack and stitch the crotch seam in one operation.

3 Turn under 1.3cm ($\frac{1}{2}$in) at pants top and tack. Turn under a further 2.5cm (1in), tack and machine, leaving a small opening for elastic.

4 Thread elastic through casing, overlap ends 1.3cm ($\frac{1}{2}$in) and stitch to secure. Complete stitching of casing.

5 Turn up pants hem and stitch as for top.

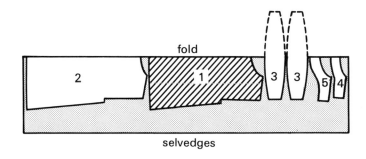

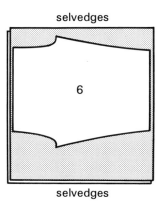

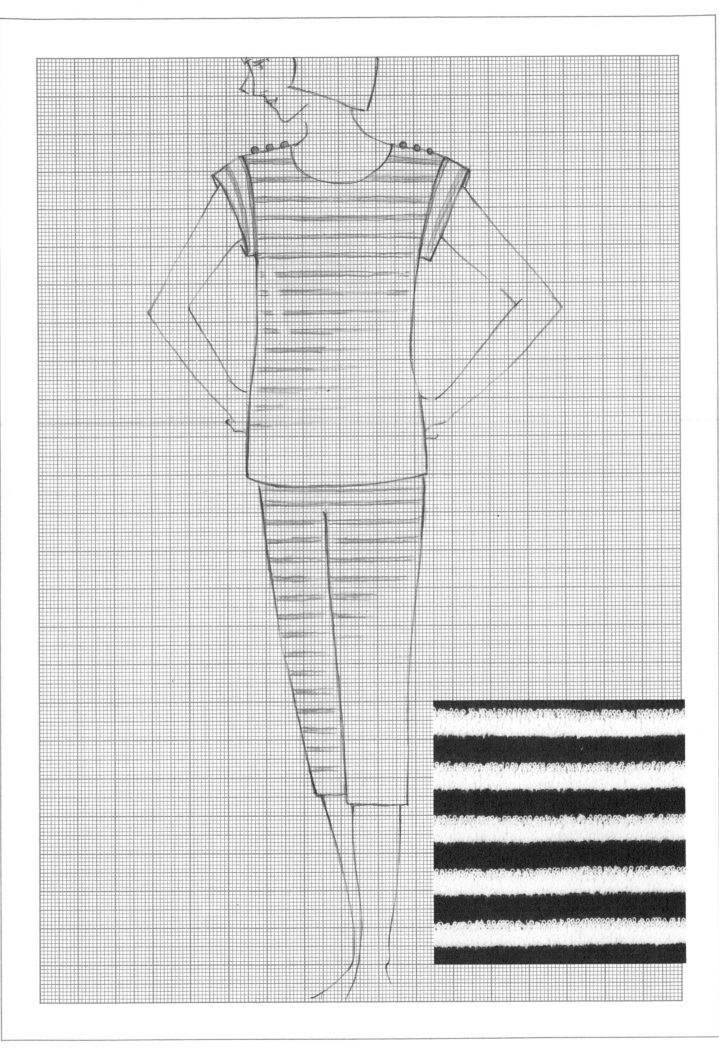

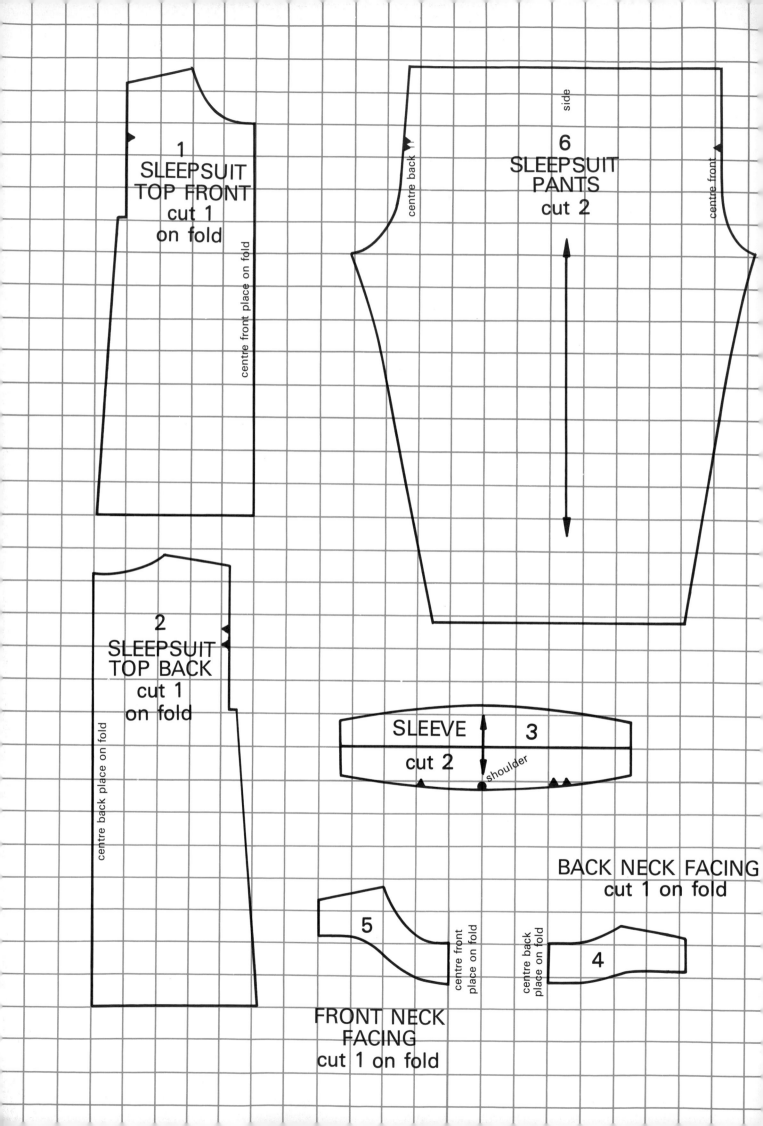

1
SLEEPSUIT
TOP FRONT
cut 1
on fold

centre front place on fold

6
SLEEPSUIT
PANTS
cut 2

side

centre back

centre front

2
SLEEPSUIT
TOP BACK
cut 1
on fold

centre back place on fold

SLEEVE **3**
cut 2
shoulder

BACK NECK FACING
cut 1 on fold

5

centre front
place on fold

centre back
place on fold

4

FRONT NECK
FACING
cut 1 on fold

Housedress

Nothing could be more simple to make than this charming housedress – there are only two pattern pieces so that even a beginner would find it easy. We have made ours in a rich figured, crêpe-backed satin and trimmed it with a pretty embroidered flower motif.

Materials

3m (3⅓yd) of 90cm (36in) wide fabric
Fabric and net-embroidered flower motif (purchased)
shirring elastic
sewing thread to match fabric
squared paper for pattern

Measurements

The pattern is given in size 12, for measurements see chart on page 123.

To make pattern

Draw up the pattern to scale from the graph pattern given here. One square represents 5cm (2in).

To adapt pattern

For size 10, cut away 1.3cm (½in) from front and back side edges.
For size 14, alter in the same places but add amounts.

To cut out

No seam allowance is included on the pattern. When cutting out add 1.5cm (⅝in) to all edges. Pin pattern pieces to fabric following the cutting layout and cut out.
Cut 2.5cm (1in) wide bias strips of fabric to bind front opening and neck edges and to make 2 50cm (20in) long ties.
Transfer all pattern markings.

To make the housedress

1 Tack and stitch flower motif to right front in position indicated on pattern. Work a second row of stitching around net area on flower. On the wrong side, cut away fabric behind net. Press flat.
2 Reinforce the lower edge of front opening with machine stitching and slash to reinforcing. *See diagram 1.* Bind opening edge with bias strip, taking 6mm (¼in) seam for machine stitch, and finishing turned over edge by hand. With right sides together, sew a tiny dart at lower edge of front-opening binding. *See diagram 2.*

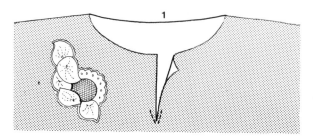

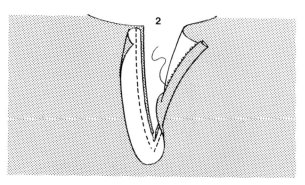

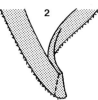

3 With right sides together, tack and stitch the front to the back at shoulder and side seams. Press seams open and neaten raw edges by hand or machine overcasting.
4 Trim seam allowance off neck edge. Bind the neck edge with bias strip as above. Make 2 rouleau ties from bias strips and sew one to each side of front opening at neck edge.
5 At the sleeve and lower-hem edges turn under 1cm (⅜in) and machine stitch close to folded edge. Trim seam allowance close to stitching. Turn under a narrow hem and sew by hand. Press all hems flat.
6 With thread on top of the machine and shirring elastic on the bobbin, work 2 rows of shirring at the waist as indicated on the pattern.

fold

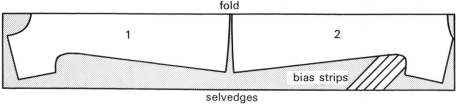

bias strips

selvedges

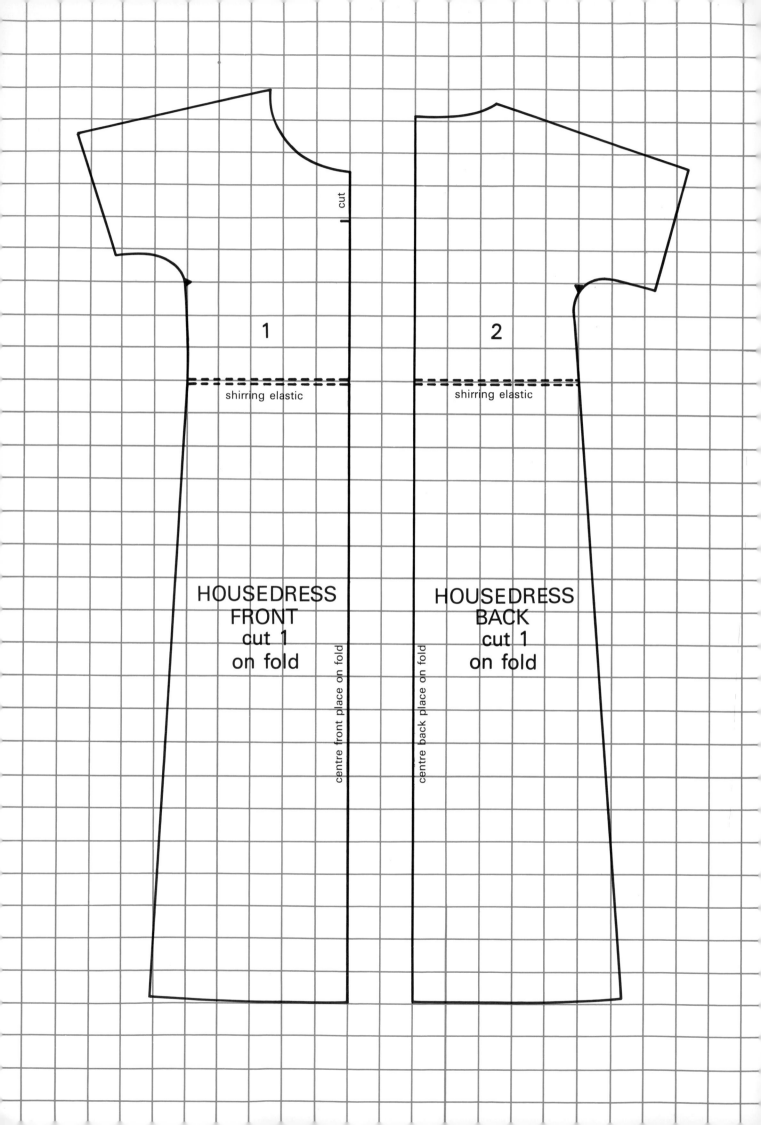

cut

1

shirring elastic

HOUSEDRESS
FRONT
cut 1
on fold

centre front place on fold

2

shirring elastic

HOUSEDRESS
BACK
cut 1
on fold

centre back place on fold

Kimono

A slinky kimono in black silk, trimmed with a contrast lace flouncing. So quick and easy to make, and lovely to wear.

Materials

3m (3⅓yd) of 90cm (36in) wide fabric (main colour)
60cm (⅔yd) of 90cm (36in) wide fabric (contrast colour)
4.8m (5⅓yd) of 5cm (2in) wide lace flouncing
sewing thread to match fabric
squared paper for pattern

Measurements

The pattern is given in size 12, for measurements see chart on page 123.

To make pattern

Draw up the pattern to scale from the graph pattern given here. One square represents 5cm (2in).

To adapt pattern

For size 10, cut away 1.3cm (½in) from the kimono front and back side and underarm edges. For size 14, alter in the same places but add amounts.

To cut out

No seam allowance is included on the pattern. When cutting out add 1.5cm (⅝in) to all seam edges and 4.5cm (1¾in) to the lower-hem edge. Pin pattern pieces to fabric following the cutting layout and cut out.
For the kimono sash cut a piece in contrast fabric 25.5cm × 181cm (10in × 71in), joining where necessary to achieve length.
Transfer all pattern markings.

To make the kimono

1 Using a french seam, join fronts to back at the shoulders. Press seams towards the back.
2 Turn under the seam allowance on the sleeve edge and tack. Place the lace flouncing just under the sleeve edge. Tack, and on the right side top stitch close to the edge. On the wrong side trim the excess seam allowance close to the stitching. *See diagram 1.*

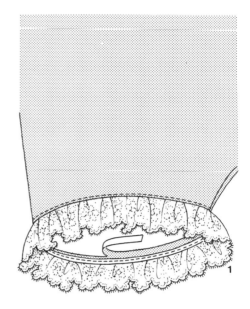

3 Using a french seam, join the fronts to the back at the side and underarms in one action. Press the seam towards the back.
4 At the lower-hem edge turn under 6mm (¼in) and then 4cm (1½in), and slipstitch hem to garment. Press hem flat.
5 At the front and neck edges, turn under the seam allowance and tack. Attach lace flouncing as for sleeve edges, turning a tiny hem on lace raw edges.
6 With right sides together, fold sash in half lengthwise and tack and stitch long and short edges, leaving an opening on long edge for turning through. Cut seam allowance across corners and turn sash to right side. Tack close to all edges and press flat. Slipstitch opening to close.
7 At side seams and at waist level, using sewing thread, work crochet chain-stitch sash carriers.

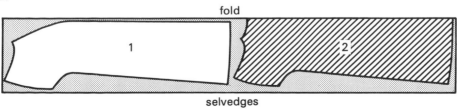

fold

1   2

selvedges

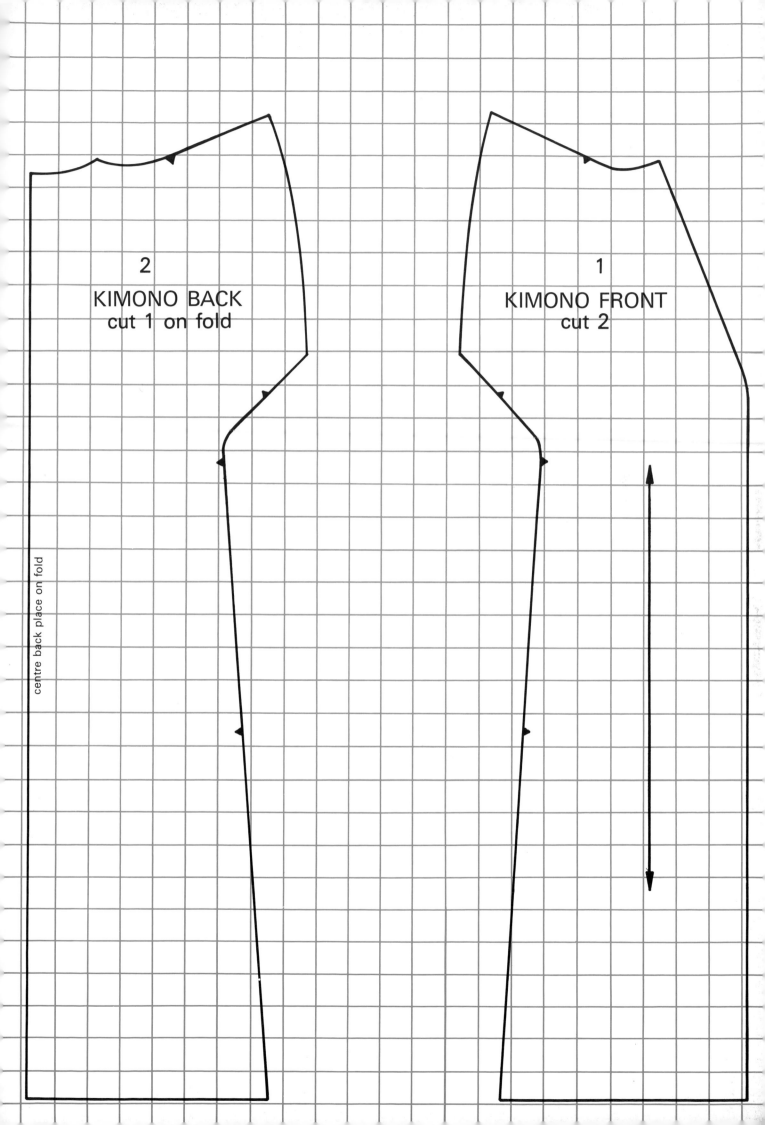

2

KIMONO BACK
cut 1 on fold

centre back place on fold

1

KIMONO FRONT
cut 2

Négligé

A very feminine négligé scattered with fur-fabric leaf shapes and with the front edges trimmed in a fluffy, downy, feather trim. The fabric is a fine polyester georgette.

Materials
2.4m (2⅔yd) of 115cm (45in) wide fabric
4.8m (5⅓yd) of feather trim
50cm (½yd) of 150cm (60in) wide fur fabric
sewing thread to match fabric
squared paper for pattern

Measurements
The pattern is given in size 12, for measurements see chart on page 123.

To make pattern
Draw up the pattern to scale from the graph pattern given here. One square represents 5cm (2in).

To adapt pattern
For size 10, cut away 1.3cm (½in) from the négligé front and back side edges and from the sleeve underarm edges.
For size 14, alter in the same places but add amounts.

To cut out
No seam allowance is included on the pattern. When cutting out add 1.5cm (⅝in) to all edges. Pin pattern pieces to fabric following the cutting layouts and cut out.
For the négligé belt cut 2 pieces of fabric 100cm × 9cm (39½in × 3½in).
Cut out 60 fur-fabric leaves with the pile running from top to bottom of each one.
Transfer all pattern markings.

To make the négligé
1 Scatter fur-fabric leaves on the right side of fabric pieces and pin in place.
Place 12 on each front, 8 on each sleeve and 20 on the back, keeping clear of the seam allowances. Using a zigzag stitch on the machine, and working on the right side, stitch leaves in place. Trim away ends of fur pile. *See diagram 1*. Using a cool iron, press flat on the wrong side.
2 Join fronts to back at shoulders with french seams. Press seam towards back.
3 Matching notches, and with dot to shoulder seam, tack and stitch the sleeve into the armhole, using a french seam. Press seam towards sleeve. Repeat for second sleeve.

1

4 Using a french seam, matching armhole seams, stitch the side and underarm seams in one action. Press seam towards back.
5 At sleeve and lower-hem edges, turn up 6mm (¼in) and then a further 1cm (⅜in) and machine. Press flat.
6 On the front and neck edges work a row of stay stitching 6mm (¼in) in from raw edge. Trim fabric close to machine stitching. Make a narrow roll-hem edge and slipstitch in place.
7 Working from the wrong side of the garment, hand sew the feather trim to neck, front and hem, and sleeve edges of garment, making joins at centre back and underarm seams.
8 With right sides together, tack and stitch centre-back seam of belt pieces. Press seam open. With right sides together, fold the belt in half lengthwise. Tack and stitch, leaving an opening on the long edge for turning through. Trim seam allowance and cut across corners. Turn belt to right side. Tack close to all edges and press flat. Slipstitch opening to close.
9 For the belt carriers cut 2 pieces of fabric 7cm × 3.2cm (2¾in × 1¼in). With right sides together, fold in half lengthwise and stitch 6mm (¼in) in from edge. Turn to right side and press flat. Fold ends under 1cm (⅜in) and sew to positions indicated on pattern at side seams.

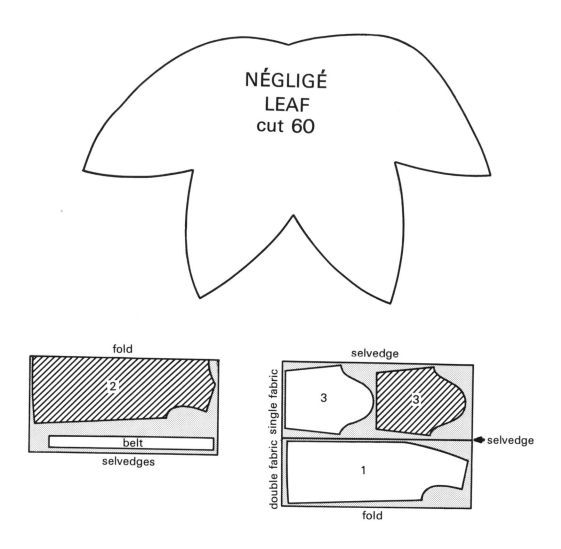

NÉGLIGÉ
LEAF
cut 60

fold

2

belt

selvedges

selvedge

double fabric   single fabric

3

3

selvedge

1

fold

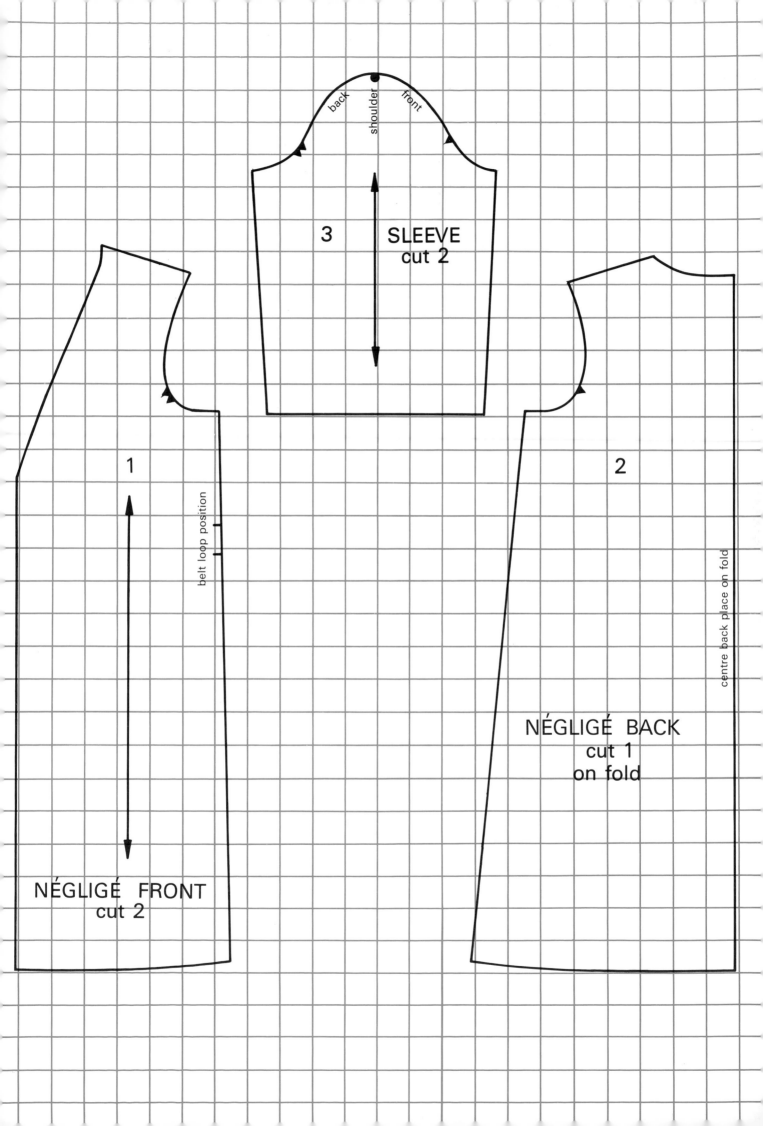

3   SLEEVE
cut 2

back   shoulder   front

1

belt loop position

NÉGLIGÉ FRONT
cut 2

2

centre back place on fold

NÉGLIGÉ BACK
cut 1
on fold

Tracksuit

A comfortable tracksuit to jog in or for simply lounging about the house. The welting can be purchased, or ribbed on a knitting machine.

Materials

4.5m (5yd) of 90cm (36in) wide stretch towelling fabric/stretch terry
2 50g (2oz) balls of Patons 4 ply Child's Play knitting yarn for ribbed welting; alternatively, use purchased welting
2.5cm (1in) wide elastic for trouser waist
2.5m ($2\frac{2}{3}$yd) of 1.3cm ($\frac{1}{2}$in) wide straight binding
sewing thread to match fabric
squared paper for pattern

Measurements

The pattern is given in size 12, for measurements see chart on page 123.

To make pattern

Draw up the pattern to scale from the graph pattern given here. One square represents 5cm (2in).

To adapt pattern

For size 10, cut away 1.3cm ($\frac{1}{2}$in) from top front and back side edges; sleeve underarm edges and trouser front and back side edges.
For size 14, alter in the same places but add amounts.

To cut out

No seam allowance is included on the pattern. When cutting out add 1cm ($\frac{3}{8}$in) to all seam edges and 5cm (2in) to trouser-waist edge.
Pin pattern pieces to fabric following the cutting layout and cut out.
Transfer all pattern markings.

Ribbed welts

On the knitting machine make a tension square 100 sts by 100 rows. The tension should be as tight as possible while allowing for stretch shown on pattern. Measure up knitted square against pattern to calculate the correct number of stitches and rows for your machine (the same for sizes 10:12:14). Knit 2 ankle ribs; 2 wrist ribs, 2 waistbands and 2 yokes.

To make tracksuit top

1   With right sides together, tack and stitch front to back at side seams. Work a second row of stitching the width of the machine foot away

from the first. Neaten raw edges by hand or machine overcasting.
2   With right sides together, tack and stitch sleeve underarm seams. Neaten as for side seams.
3   With right sides together, pin yoke to top edge of front, easing in fullness. Tack and stitch, stretching the seam as you do so. Neaten seam edge as before. Press seam downwards. On right side, top stitch close to the seamline to hold seam allowance down. *See diagram 1.*

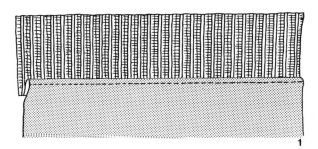

4   Stretch back-yoke rib to 58cm (23in) and pin down on ironing board. Lay yoke shoulder pattern piece on top and, in contrast thread, tack outline onto rib. Stitch back yoke to back as instructed for front yoke.
5   Using wool, hand stitch overlapped front and back yokes together at shoulders. *See diagram 2.*

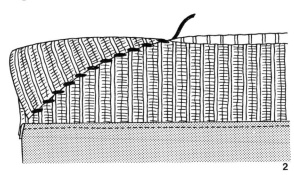

6   With right sides together, matching underarm seams and notches, tack and stitch sleeves into armholes. Neaten seam as above.
7   Using wool, hand stitch seams on wrist and waist ribs. With right sides together, matching seams, tack and stitch the ribs to sleeve and hem edges, stretching the ribbing to fit. Press the seam allowance upwards and on the right side top stitch close to the seam.

To make trousers

1 With right sides together, tack and stitch inside-leg seams. Neaten raw edges together by hand or machine overcasting. Press seams towards back and, on right side, top stitch the width of the machine foot away from the seam to hold seam allowance in place.

2 With right sides together, matching notches and inside-leg seams, tack and stitch the crotch seam. Reinforce the crotch seam to prevent it stretching in wear by tacking straight binding along seamline. Stitch close to edges. *See diagram 3.*

3 With right sides together, tack and stitch side seams. Neaten and top stitch seams as above.

4 Attach ankle ribs as instructed for wrist ribs.

5 At trouser-waist edge turn under 1.3cm ($\frac{1}{2}$in) and then a further 4cm ($1\frac{1}{2}$in). Tack and machine, leaving an opening for threading elastic through. Cut a piece of elastic to fit the waist comfortably plus 1.3cm ($\frac{1}{2}$in); thread this into waist casing. Overlap ends 1.3cm ($\frac{1}{2}$in) and stitch securely. Slipstitch opening to close.

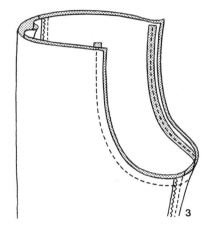

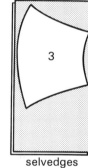

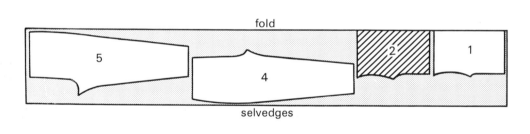

Towelling/Terry cloth bathrobe

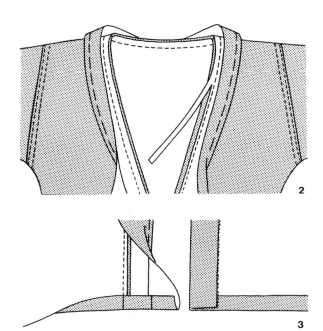

This bathrobe has deep-cut armholes with sleeves that are shaped to fit. There is a narrow band at front and neck edges, and it has deep pockets. The fronts wrap across and are held with a soft tie belt. We have made it in a fabric ideal for the beach too.

Materials
3.8m (4¼yd) of 90cm (36in) wide woven towelling fabric/terry cloth
sewing thread to match fabric
squared paper for pattern

Measurements
The pattern is given in size 12, for measurements see chart on page 123.

To make pattern
Draw up the pattern to scale from the graph pattern given here. One square represents 5cm (2in).

To adapt pattern
For size 10, cut away 1.3cm (½in) from front and back side edges and from front and back sleeve-underarm edges.
For size 14, alter in the same places but add amounts.

To cut out
No seam allowance is included on the pattern. When cutting out add 1.5cm (⅝in) to all seam edges and 2cm (¾in) to sleeve and lower-hem edges. Pin pattern pieces to fabric following the cutting layout and cut out.
For the bathrobe belt cut 1 piece 11.5cm × 181cm (4½in × 71½in).
Transfer all pattern markings.

To make the bathrobe
1 With right sides together, fold each pocket piece in half. Tack and stitch raw edges together, leaving a 10cm (4in) opening on one edge. Cut seam allowance across corners and turn pockets to right side. Tack close to all edges and press flat. Slipstitch opening to close.
2 Tack pockets to robe fronts in positions indicated on pattern and top stitch in place. Press flat.
3 Using a flat-fell seam, matching notches, stitch the front sleeves to the front armholes and the back sleeves to the back armholes. Press flat. *See diagram 1.*
4 Using a flat-fell seam stitch the fronts to the back at the shoulders, also at the side and

underarms in one action. Press all seams flat.
5 At the sleeve and lower-hem edges turn under 6mm (¼in) and then a further 1.3cm (½in) and machine. Press hems flat.
6 With right sides together, tack and stitch the front bands to the back neck band. Press seams open. Repeat for band facing.
7 With right sides together, matching shoulder seams, tack and stitch the front and back neck band to the front and back neck-band facing. Grade the seam allowance and turn to the right side. Tack close to the stitched edge and press flat.
8 With right sides together, matching shoulder seams and notches, tack and stitch the front and back neck band to the robe. Press the seam into the band. Grade the seam allowance. *See diagram 2.* Turn under the seam allowance on the band facing and lower edges, and tack. Slipstitch to stitching line and slipstitch ends together at hem edge. Press band flat. *See diagram 3.*

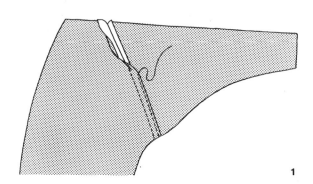

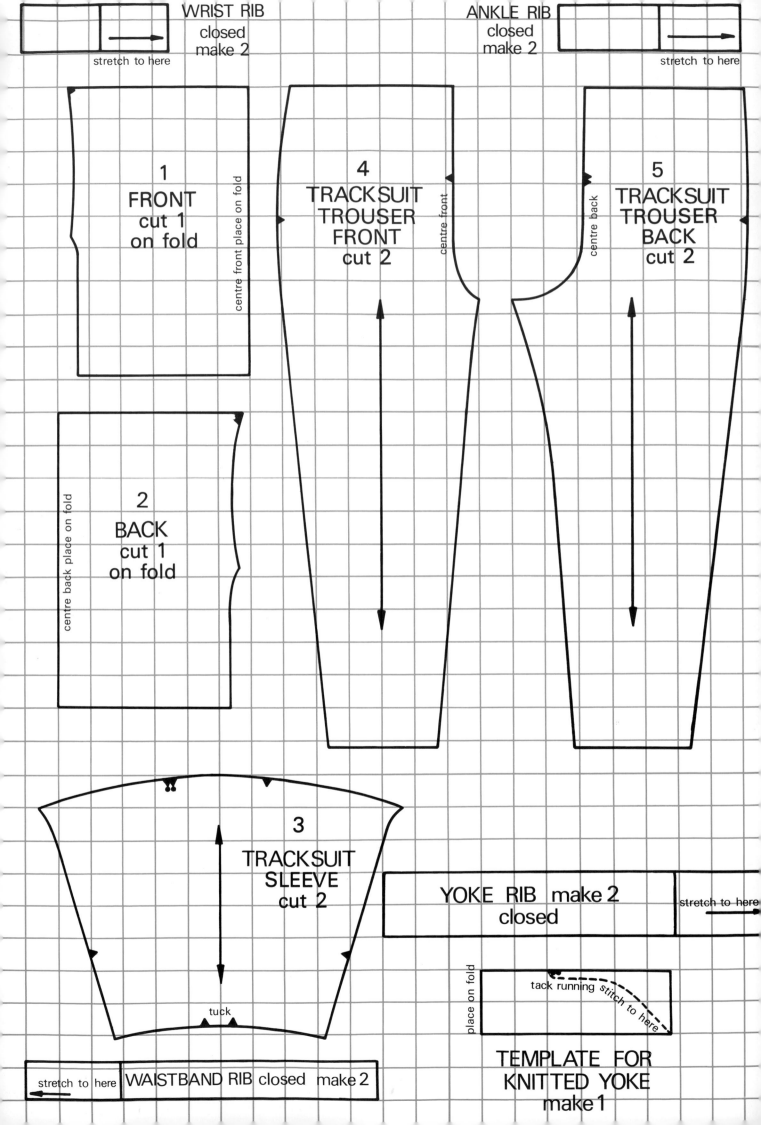

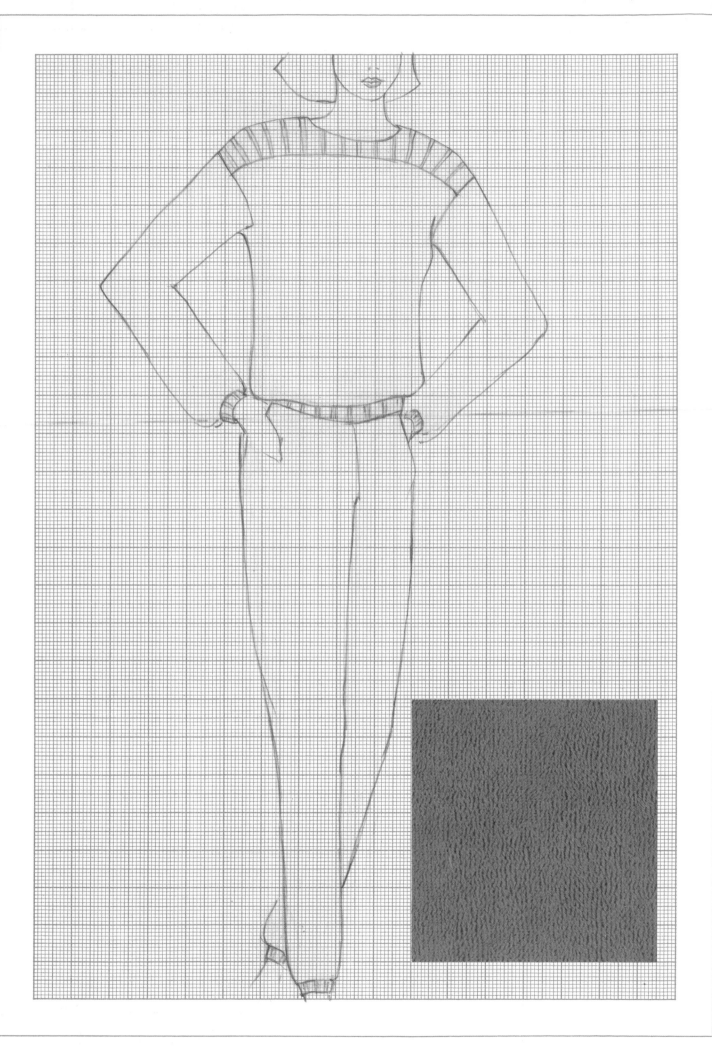

9 With right sides together, fold the belt in half lengthwise and stitch the short and long edges, leaving an opening on the long edge for turning through. Cut seam allowance across corners and turn belt to right side. Tack close to all edges and press flat. Slipstitch opening to close.

10 Using sewing thread, make a crochet–chain or buttonhole-loop belt carrier at waist level on side seams.

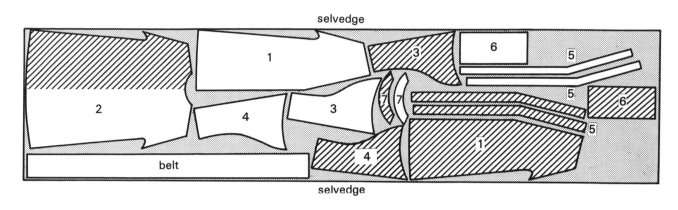

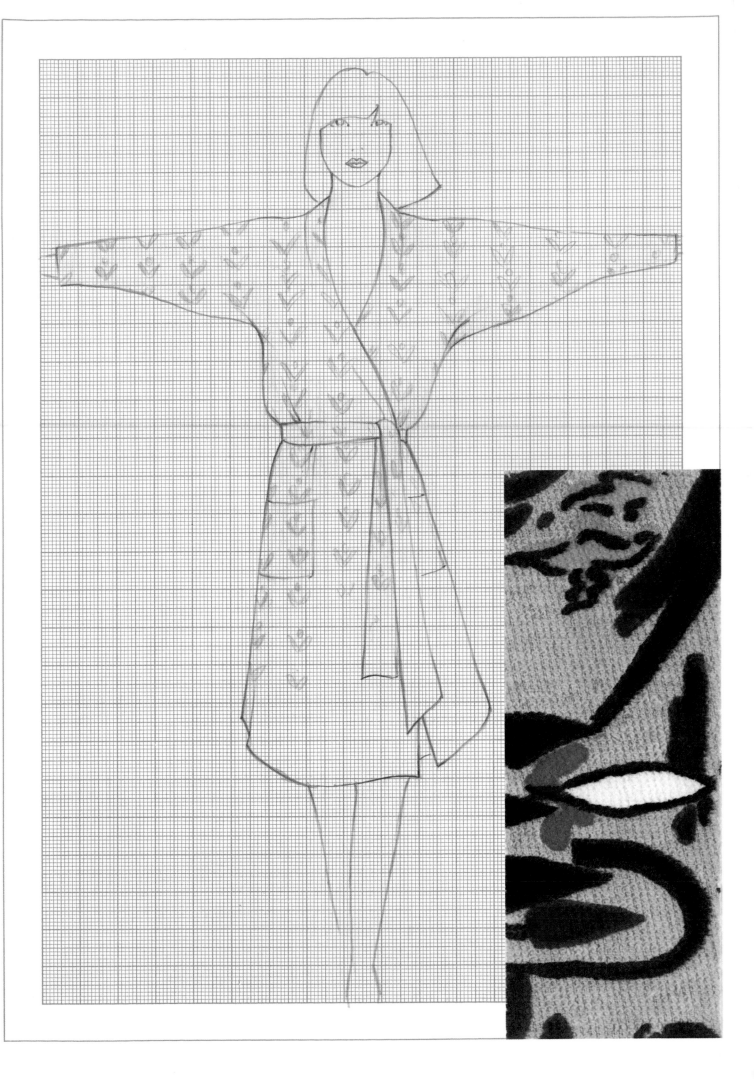

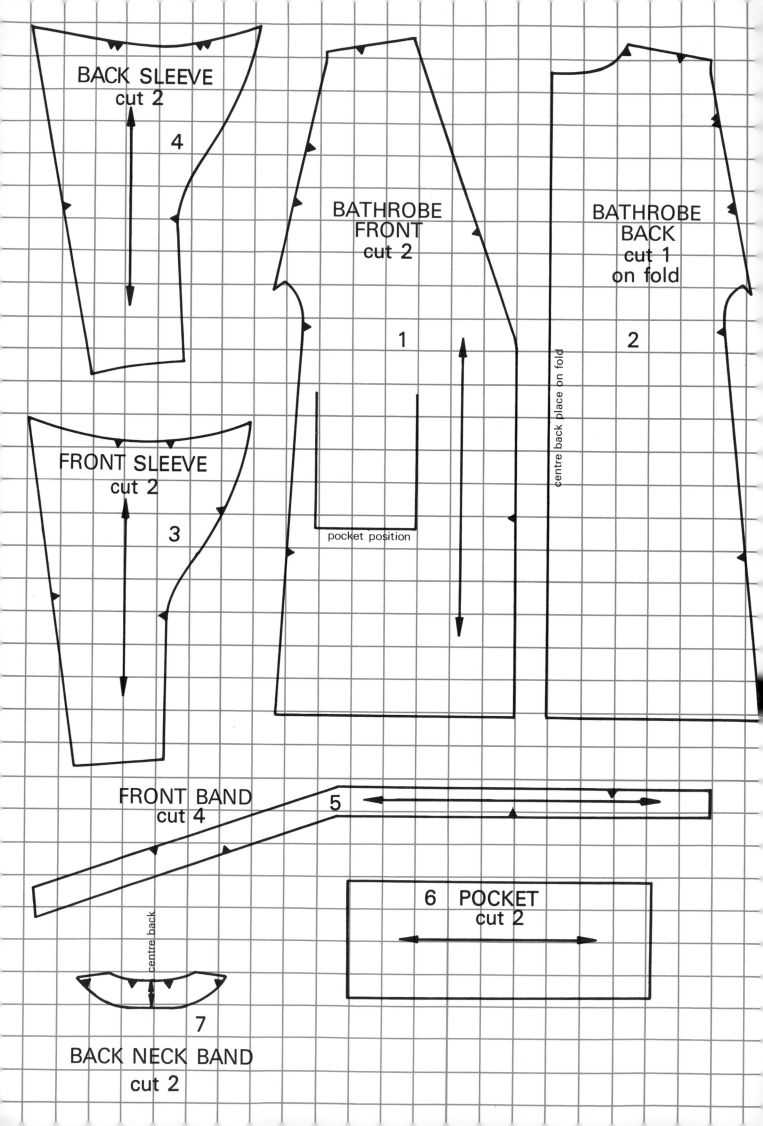

Summer dressing-gown

This lovely full length, wrap-over dressing-gown made in heavy crêpe-backed figured satin has delicate lace yokes and trimming at sleeve edges. The soft shawl collar is flattering to wear.

Materials
3.5m (3⅞yd) of 115cm (45in) wide fabric
1.5m (1⅔yd) of 15cm (6in) wide lace edging
sewing thread to match fabric
squared paper for pattern

Measurements
The pattern is given in size 12, for measurements see chart on page 123.

To make pattern
Draw up the pattern to scale from the graph pattern given here. One square represents 5cm (2in).

To adapt pattern
For size 10, cut away 1.3cm (½in) from front and back side edges and sleeve underarm edges. For size 14, alter in the same places but add amounts.

To cut out
No seam allowance is included on the pattern. When cutting out add 1.5cm (⅝in) to all seam edges and 7.5cm (3in) to the hem edge.
Pin pattern pieces to fabric following the cutting layout and cut out.
For the belt, cut a piece of fabric 160cm × 10cm (63in × 4in).
Transfer all pattern markings.

To make the dressing-gown
1   Reinforce the inner corners on fronts and facings at circles. Snip into corners. *See diagram 1.*

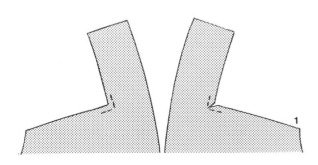

2   With right sides together, tack and stitch fronts together at collar centre-back seam. Press seam open. Join the front facings together in the same way. Neaten the inner raw edges of the facings by hand or machine overcasting.

3   With right sides together, tack and stitch the centre-back seam. Press seam open.

4   With right sides together, tack and stitch the front yokes to the back yokes at the shoulder seams. Work a second row of stitching 6mm (¼in) away from the first. Trim seam allowance close to stitching and overcast raw edges by hand or machine.

5   Work two rows of gathering stitches between the notches on gown fronts.

6   Lay back lace yoke to overlap right side of back yoke seamline by 1.5cm (⅝in). Tack and stitch on seamline. *See diagram 2.*

Press seam away from yoke and neaten raw edge by hand or machine overcasting. On the right side, top stitch close to seamline to hold seam allowance down. Press flat.

7   With right sides together, matching centre backs, tack and stitch gown back and yokes to collar neckline between circles. *See diagram 3.* Press the seam towards the collar.

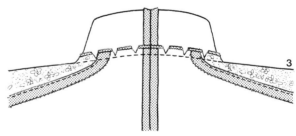

8   Lay the front lace yoke to overlap right side of front yoke seamline by 1.5cm (⅝in). Pin in place, pulling up gathers. Distribute gathers evenly. Tack and machine. *See diagram 4.* Press the seam away from the yoke. Neaten raw edges as above. On the right side, top stitch close to seamline to hold seam allowance down.

9   With right sides together, matching notches and with circle to shoulder seam, tack and stitch sleeves into armholes. Press seam towards sleeve.

79

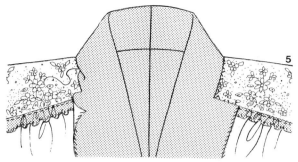

At the neck and yoke seam edges, turn under the seam allowance and slipstitch to stitching line. Press flat. *See diagram 5.*

Work a second row of stitching 6mm ($\frac{1}{4}$in) away from the first. Trim seam allowance close to stitching and overcast raw edges by hand or machine.

10 With right sides together, having straight edges level, stitch lace edging to sleeve-hem edges. Press seam towards sleeve. Neaten raw edges as before. On the right side top stitch close to the seam edge to hold the seam in place.

11 With right sides together, matching armhole seams, tack and stitch the side and underarm seams in one operation. Neaten the raw edges together as above. Press the seams towards the back.

12 With right sides together, matching centre backs and notches, tack and stitch the facing to the gown collar and front edges. Grade seam allowance and notch curves. Turn to right side. Tack close to stitched edges and press flat.

13 Neaten the hem raw edge by hand or machine overcasting. Open out the facing, turn up hem and catch-stitch in place.

14 Catch-stitch facing inner edge to garment, and slipstitch hem edges together. Press hem flat.

15 With right sides together, fold belt in half lengthways. Tack and stitch long and short edges, leaving an opening on the long edge for turning through. Cut seam allowance across corners and turn belt to right side. Tack close to all edges and press flat. Slipstitch opening to close.

16 At the side seams make crochet-chain or buttonhole-stitch belt carriers.

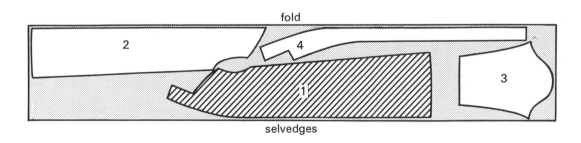

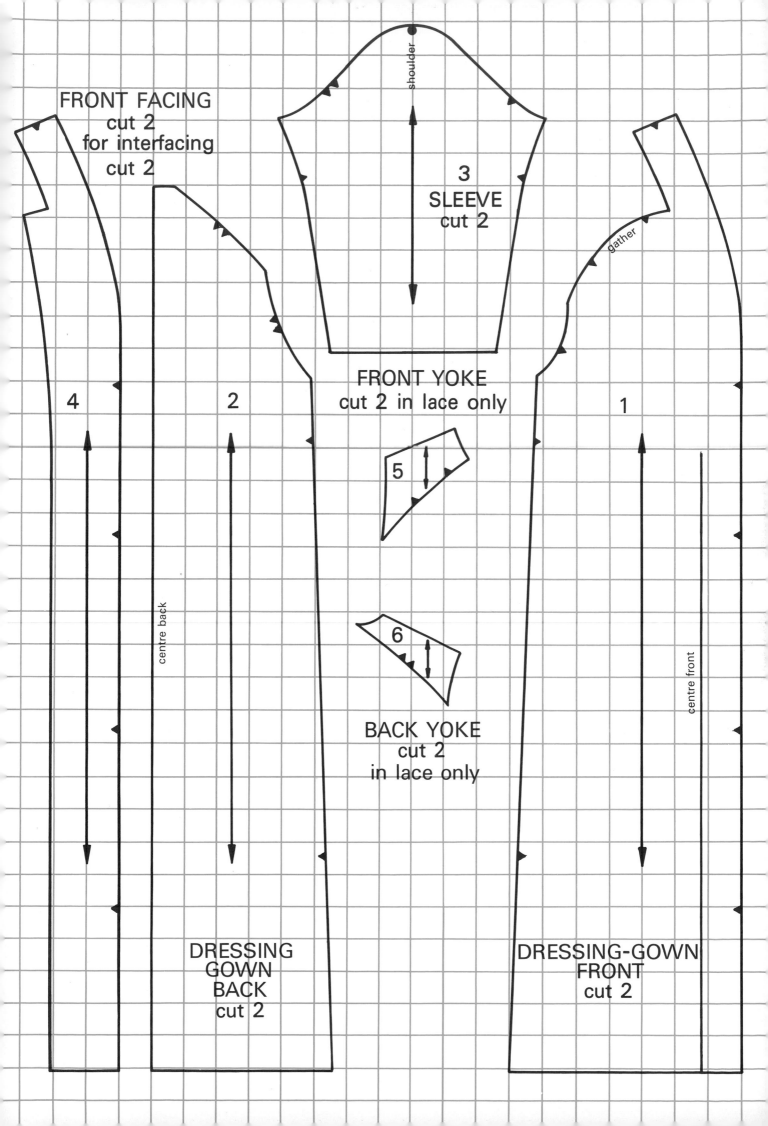

FRONT FACING
cut 2
for interfacing
cut 2

4

3
SLEEVE
cut 2

shoulder

gather

2

FRONT YOKE
cut 2 in lace only

1

5

centre back

6

BACK YOKE
cut 2
in lace only

centre front

DRESSING
GOWN
BACK
cut 2

DRESSING-GOWN
FRONT
cut 2

Quilted dressing-gown

This beautiful quilted dressing-gown looks richly different with its contrast lining and piping. Good looks and warmth are combined here to make a practical, washable garment.

Materials

4.5m (5yd) of 90cm (36in) wide quilted fabric
5m (5½yd) of 90cm (36in) wide figured polyester (pink) for lining
20cm (¼yd) of 90cm (36in) wide black figured polyester for ties
5m (5½yd) of piping cord
sewing thread to match fabrics
black machine embroidery thread
squared paper for pattern

Measurements

The pattern is given in size 12, for measurements see chart on page 123.

To make pattern

Draw up the pattern to scale from the graph pattern given here. One square represents 5cm (2in).

To adapt pattern

For size 10, cut away 1.3cm (½in) from front and back side edges and from sleeve front and back underarm edges.
For size 14, alter in the same places but add amounts.

To cut out

No seam allowance is included on the pattern. When cutting out add 1.5cm (⅝in) to all edges. Pin pattern pieces to fabric following the cutting layout and cut out.
For the dressing-gown ties cut 2 pieces of fabric each in pink and black lining fabric measuring 47cm × 8.2cm (18½in × 3¼in).
Cut 3.5cm (1⅜in) wide bias strips from lining to cover piping cord.
Transfer all pattern markings.

To make dressing-gown

1   Join bias strips to required length to cover piping cord. Press all seams open. Insert piping cord in centre, fold edge and tack close to cord. *See diagram 1.*
2   With right sides together fold ties in half lengthwise, tack and stitch, leaving one short end open and stitching other short end diagonally. Trim seam allowance at shaped end. Turn to right side, tack close to all edges and press flat.

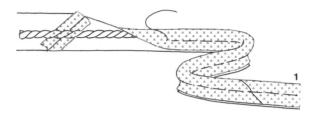

3   With right sides together, tack and stitch collar lining to front-band lining pieces. Press seams open.
4   Having raw edges level, tack piping to outer edges of collar and front-band linings, inserting one black tie under the piping and placing one pink one on top in position indicated on pattern. *See diagram 2.*

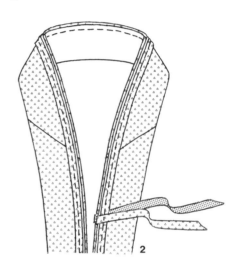

5   Tack piping to shoulder seam of back sleeve, taking it up to the neck. With right sides together, tack and stitch the front sleeve to the back sleeve along the shoulder seam using a piping or zipper foot on the machine. Repeat for sleeve linings, omitting piping.
6   With right sides together, tack and stitch pockets to front and back side seams in positions indicated on the pattern.
7   Spread out each piece of lining, wrong side of lining to wrong side of the garment. On right side, pin together at each alternate corner of quilting, leaving 5cm (2in) free on all edges and around pocket area on fronts.
8   Using zigzag on the machine with the stitch length set at 'O' and black machine embroidery thread, work 10 to 12 stitches over each marked corner. *See diagram 3.*
9   Pin all lining pieces away from seam edges. With right sides together, matching notches and dots, tack and stitch the side seams from dot to

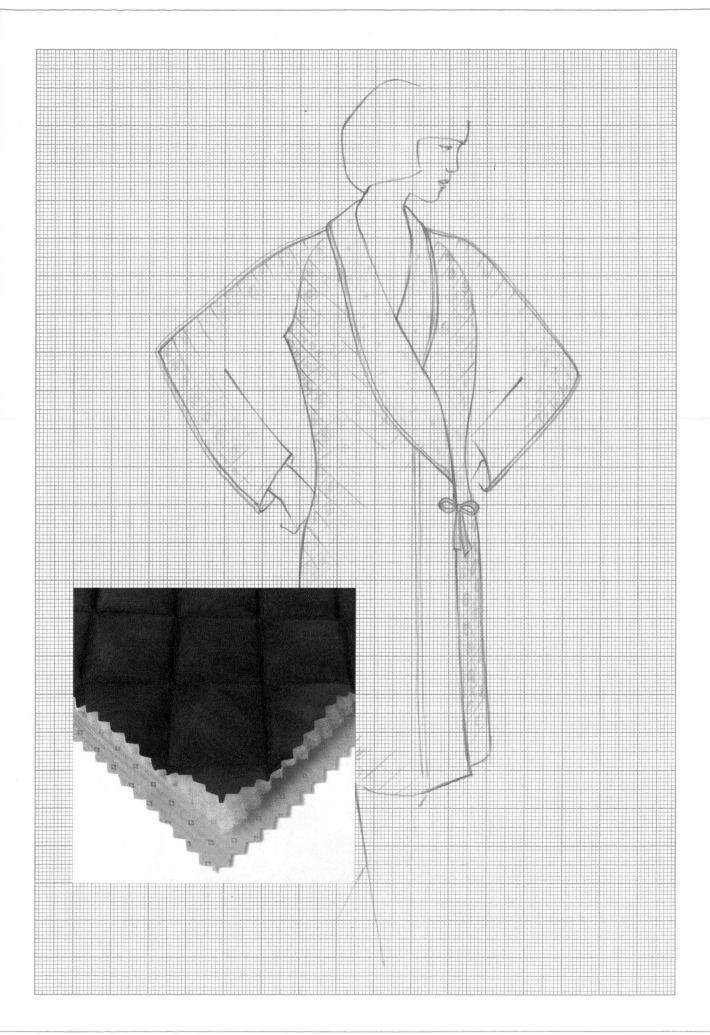

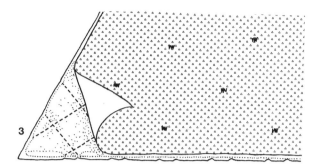

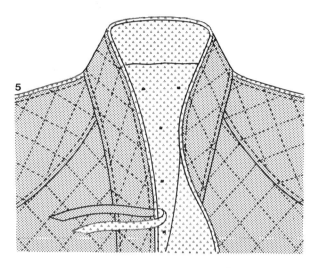

front bands, enclosing the piping as you do so and using a piping foot on the machine. *See diagram 4.*

12 On the right side, top stitch 6mm ($\frac{1}{4}$in) from piped edge on quilting, to hold seam allowances in place, leaving lining free. *See diagram 5.*

hem and from dot to underarm. Stitch from dot to dot round pocket edge. Tuck pocket into space left between lining and quilting at front and attach in two or three places to match rest of embroidery. Press the side seams towards the front and, on right side, top stitch the width of the machine foot away from the seam.

10 With right sides together, tack and stitch the underarm seam. Top stitch seam as for side seams.
With right sides together, tack and stitch sleeves into armholes. Press seams towards sleeve and top stitch.

11 With right sides together, tack and stitch collar and front bands lining to the collar and

13 Turn up and tack sleeve and lower hem edges 1.5cm ($\frac{5}{8}$in) and, on right side top stitch 6mm ($\frac{1}{4}$in) from the edge.

14 Unpin lining round edges. At each seam, turn under the seam allowance on one raw edge and overlap this on the other seam allowance. Slipstitch seam. Catch lining to quilting as before at 10cm (4in) intervals along seams, leaving 5cm (2in) free at hem edges.

15 Turn under lining at hem edge and slipstitch in place.

16 Turn under seam allowance on collar and front-band lining and slipstitch to stitching line. Catch lining to quilting as before.

17 Turn in ends of remaining ties and tack black one to pink side and pink one to black side in position indicated on pattern.

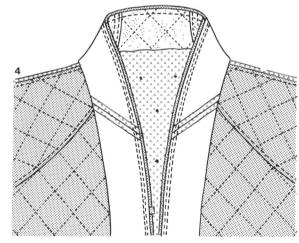

FABRIC

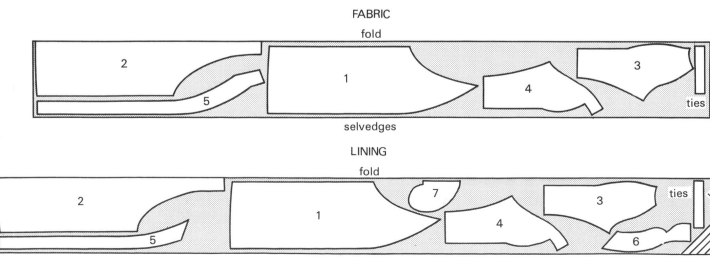

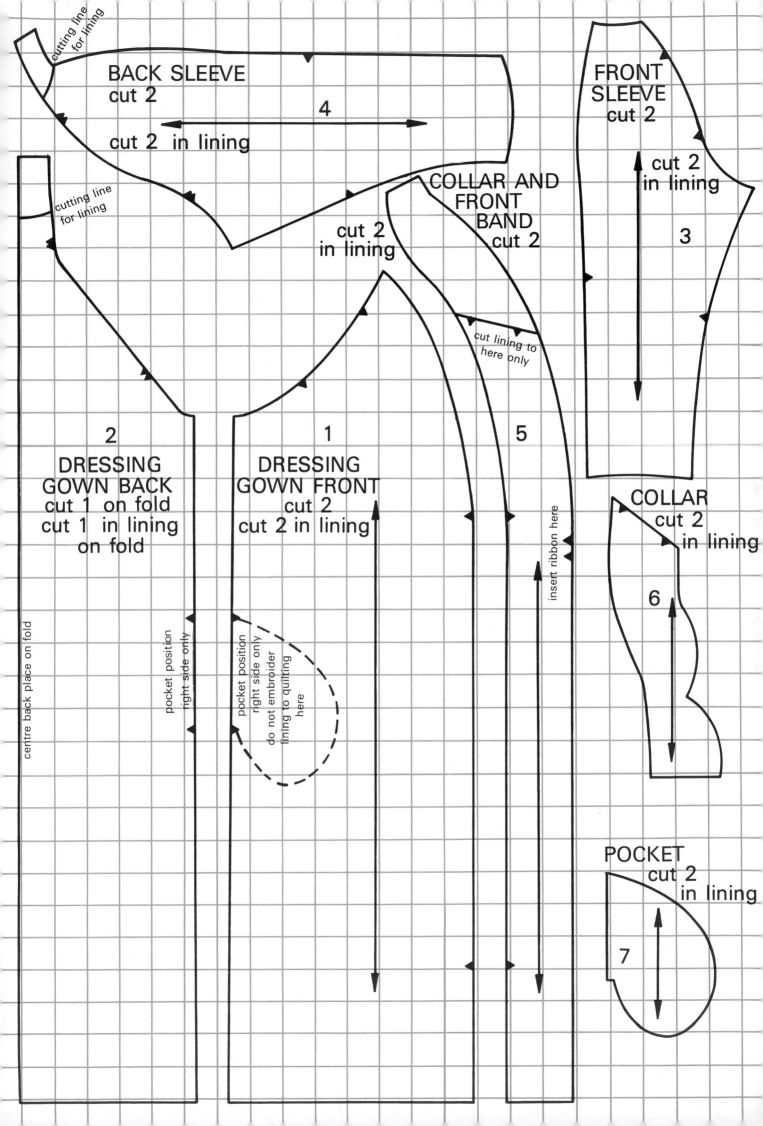

Feel your best in pure silk undies trimmed with toning lace. They are quick and easy to make and so pretty too.

Materials

1m (1⅛yd) of 90cm (36in) wide silk crêpe-de-chine

2.6m (2⅞yd) of 3.5cm (1⅜in) wide nylon lace

60cm (⅔yd) of 6mm (¼in) wide elastic

40cm (½yd) of 1cm (⅜in) wide elastic

20cm (¼yd) of 2.5cm (1in) wide elastic

30cm (⅓yd) of 6mm (¼in) wide ribbon

10cm (⅛yd) of 2.5cm (1in) wide petersham ribbon

2 hooks and bars (size 1)

sewing thread to match fabric and lace

squared paper for patterns

Measurements

The pattern is given in size 12, for measurements see chart on page 123.

To make pattern

Draw up the pattern to scale from the graph pattern given here. One square represents 5cm (2in).

To adapt pattern

For size 10, cut away 6mm (¼in) from bra cup centre front and side edges and pleat away 2.5cm (1in) at sides of knickers.

For size 14, alter in the same places but add amounts.

To cut out

No seam allowance is included on the pattern. When cutting out add 1.5cm (⅝in) to all edges. Pin pattern pieces to fabric following the cutting layouts and cut out.

Transfer all pattern markings.

To make bra

1   With right sides together, matching notches, tack and stitch the centre-front and side-front bra cup and bra cup facing sections together, without stretching the seam as you stitch. Press seams open.

2   With right sides together, place bra cup and bra cup facing sections together and tack along lower edge. Stitch and trim seam allowance to 6mm (¼in). Turn to right side, tack close to stitched edges and press flat.

3   Machine 1cm (⅜in) from lower edge on each bra cup to form casing. *See diagram 1.* For size 10,

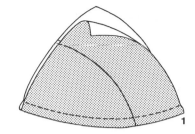

cut two strips of 1cm (⅜in) wide elastic 13cm (5⅛in) long; for size 12, 14cm (5½in) long and for size 14, 15cm (5⅞in) long. Insert elastic into casing and secure ends firmly.

4   Using the lace template as a guide, match lace pattern at front and make tucks in lace where necessary. Tack lace to seamline of each bra cup. Work a line of straight stitches and then stitch over with a narrow zigzag to secure in place. *See diagram 2.*

5   Join side sections to side section facings at top and bottom seamlines. Trim seam allowance to 6mm (¼in) and turn to right side. Tack close to stitched edges and press flat.

6   Place bra cup with lace edge on seamline of side section. Tack and stitch lace in place. *See diagram 3.* Trim excess seam allowance close to stitching. At open end, turn in seam allowance and tack.

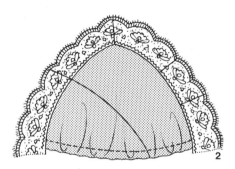

7   Tack and stitch the back casing sections together, leaving open at short ends. Trim seam allowance and turn to right side. Tack close to

stitched edges and press flat. Cut 2 pieces 2.5cm (1in) wide elastic in the following lengths: for size 10, 8.5cm ($3\frac{3}{8}$in); for size 12, 10cm (4in); for size 14, 11.5cm ($4\frac{1}{2}$in).

8 Slot elastic into casing and secure at one end. At the other, turn in seam allowance and tack, catching elastic at the same time. Insert raw edge into back bra section, tack and machine in position. *See diagram 4.*

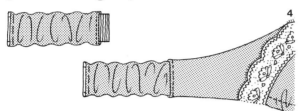

9 Make 2 short 2.5cm (1in) wide tabs reinforced with double petersham ribbon and insert in the centre back casing, leaving 1.3cm ($\frac{1}{2}$in) showing. Machine in place. Sew on hooks and bars to close. *See diagram 5.*

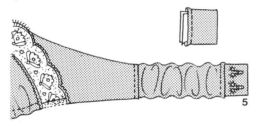

10 For shoulder-straps and centre-front join, cut 2 strips of fabric on the straight of grain 50 × 3.5cm ($19\frac{3}{4}$ × $1\frac{3}{8}$in) and 1 strip 6 × 3.5cm ($2\frac{3}{8}$ × $1\frac{3}{8}$in).
With right sides together, fold strips in half and stitch 6mm ($\frac{1}{4}$in) from folded edge. Trim seam allowance to 6mm ($\frac{1}{4}$in) and turn to right side. Press flat.

11 Place the bra cups with front lace edges meeting over the short strip and zigzag stitch in place.

12 Attach strap commencing from top of fabric section of bra cup and stitch to back of lace. Adjusting length, stitch strap to join of elastic casing at back. *See diagram 6.*

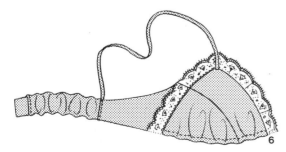

To make french knickers/tap pants

1 With right sides together, tack and stitch centre-front and centre-back seams. Press seams open.

2 Neaten centre-front and centre-back edge by hand or machine overcasting.

3 With right sides together, tack and stitch crotch seam. Neaten raw edges and press seam open.

4 Pin and tack lace to seamline on lower edge from front to back (around side of body first) through crotch seam and finally overlapping at front. *See diagram 7.* Pin and stitch tucks where necessary. Stitch lace in place with a line of straight stitching covered by zigzag stitches. Press flat.
On the wrong side, trim excess seam allowance close to stitching.

5 On knickers/pants top, turn under 6mm ($\frac{1}{4}$in) and then a further 1cm ($\frac{3}{8}$in). Tack and stitch, leaving a small opening at the centre back.

6 Cut a piece of elastic to fit the waist comfortably plus 6mm ($\frac{1}{4}$in). Insert elastic in casing. Overlap ends 6mm ($\frac{1}{4}$in) and sew together. Slipstitch opening to close.

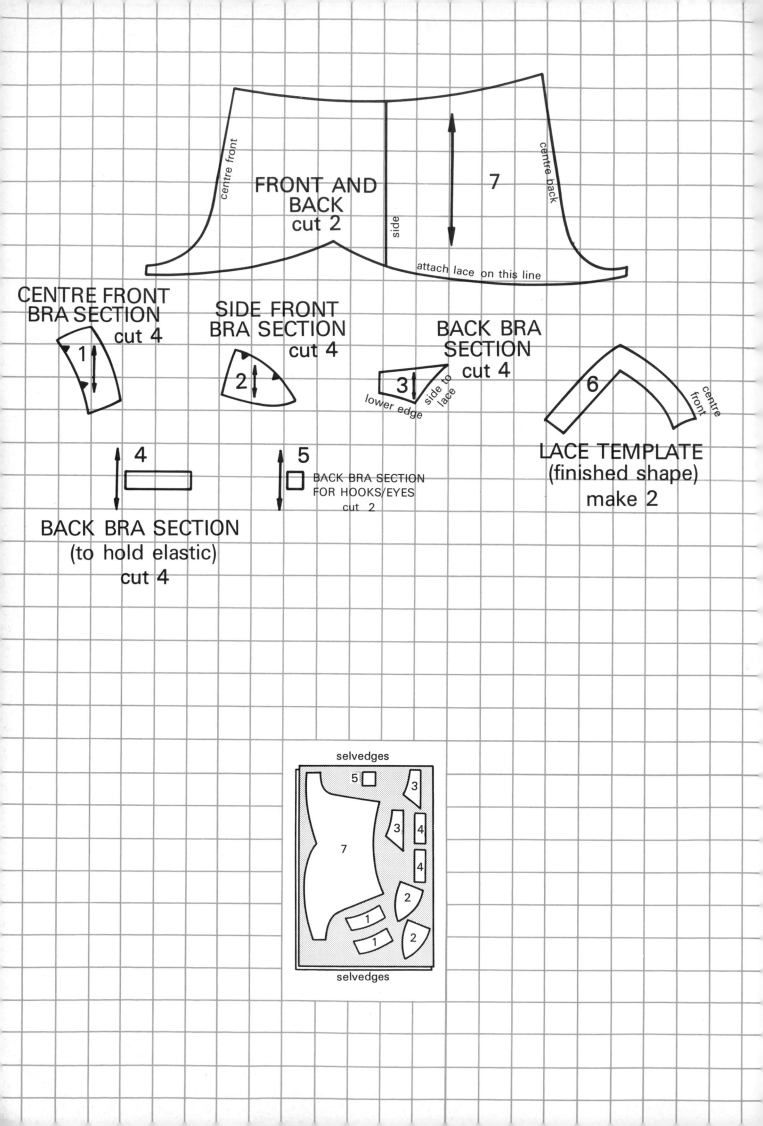

centre front

FRONT AND
BACK
cut 2

7

side

centre back

attach lace on this line

CENTRE FRONT
BRA SECTION
cut 4

1

SIDE FRONT
BRA SECTION
cut 4

2

BACK BRA
SECTION
cut 4

3

lower edge

side to lace

6

centre
front

LACE TEMPLATE
(finished shape)
make 2

4

5

BACK BRA SECTION
FOR HOOKS/EYES
cut 2

BACK BRA SECTION
(to hold elastic)
cut 4

selvedges

5

3

3

4

7

4

2

1

1

2

selvedges

Camisole

A pretty, cool-looking camisole top made in fine polyester/cotton lawn and trimmed with lace and ribbon.

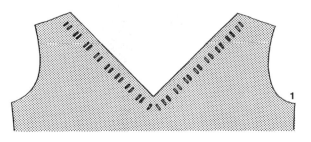

Materials
1m (1⅛yd) of 90cm (36in) wide fabric
2.1m (2¼yd) of narrow lace trimming
1m (1⅛yd) of 6mm (¼in) wide satin ribbon
sewing thread to match fabric
squared paper for pattern

Measurements
The pattern is given in size 12, for measurements see chart on page 123.

To make pattern
Draw up the pattern to scale from the graph pattern given here. One square represents 5cm (2in).

To adapt pattern
For size 10, cut away 1.3cm (½in) from the camisole front and back side edges.
For size 14, alter in the same places but add amounts.

To cut out
No seam allowance is included on the pattern.
When cutting out add 1.5cm (⅝in) to all edges.
Pin pattern pieces to fabric following the cutting layout and cut out.
Transfer all pattern markings.

To make the camisole
1   Work 1.3cm (½in) buttonholes at positions indicated round front and back neckline. Press flat. *See diagram 1.*
2   Using french seams, join front to back at sides and shoulders. Press seams towards the back.

3   Turn under seam allowance at neck and sleeve edges and tack. Snip seam allowance to lie flat where necessary.
4   Tack lace trimming to wrong side of neck and armhole edges, making joins at underarms and centre back. On the right side, top stitch close to the edge to secure lace. Press flat. On the wrong side, trim excess fabric close to stitching. *See diagram 2.*

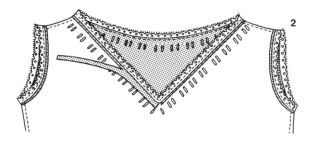

5   Turn up hem edge 6mm (¼in) and then a further 6mm (¼in) and slipstitch by hand. Press hem flat.
6   Thread ribbon through buttonholes and tie in bow at centre front.

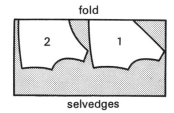

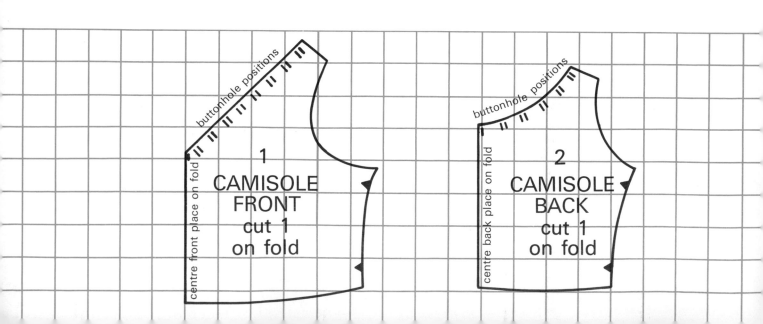

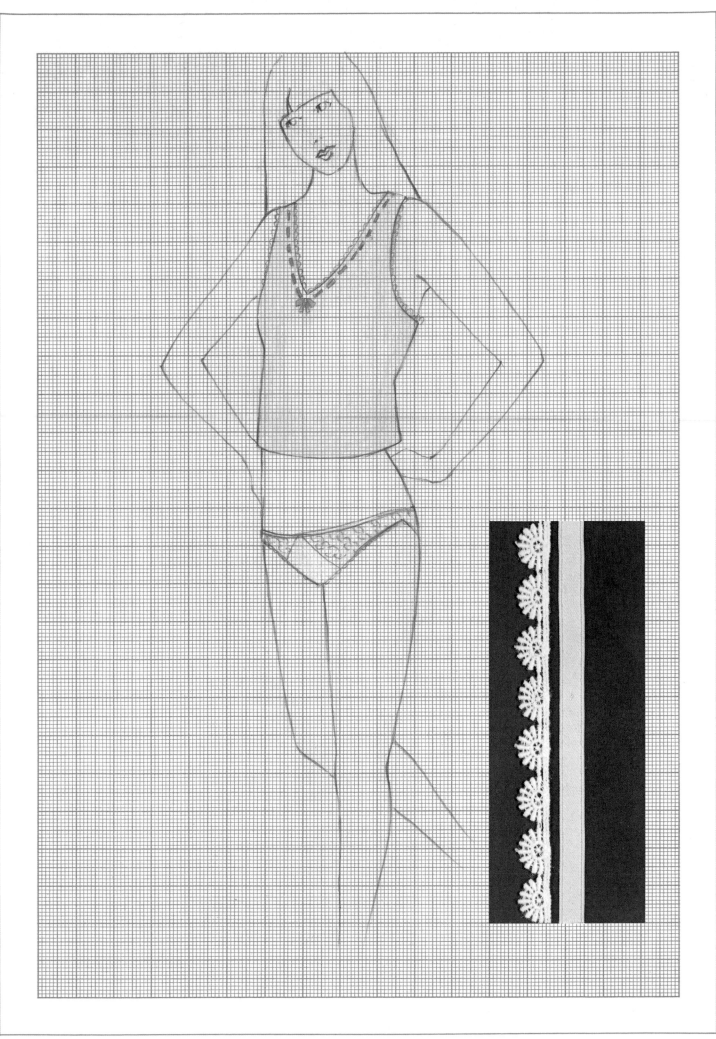

Petticoat

A pretty princess line slip made in and trimmed with broderie anglaise. It has a dainty petal-scalloped hem and narrow ribbon shoulder-straps.

Materials

1.8m (2yd) of 90cm (36in) wide fabric
1.2m (1⅓yd) of 4cm (1½in) wide broderie anglaise edging
1m (1⅛yd) of 6mm (¼in) wide satin ribbon
1 card of bias binding to match fabric
sewing thread to match fabric
squared paper for pattern

Measurements

The pattern is given in size 12, for measurements see chart on page 123.

To make pattern

Draw up the pattern to scale from the graph pattern given here. One square represents 2.5cm (1in).

To adapt pattern

For size 10, cut away 1.3cm (½in) from front and back side edges.
For size 14, alter in the same places but add amounts.

To cut out

No seam allowance is included on the pattern. When cutting out add 1.5cm (⅝in) to all edges. Pin pattern pieces to fabric following the cutting layout and cut out.
Transfer all pattern markings.

To make the petticoat

1 With right sides together, matching notches, tack and stitch the side-back panels to the centre-back panel and the side-front panels to the centre-front panel.
2 With right sides together, matching notches, tack and stitch the front to the back at the side seams.
3 Neaten all seam edges by working a second row of stitching the width of the machine foot away from the first. Trim seam allowance close to second row of stitching and overcast raw edges by hand or machine.
Press side seams towards the back and press front and back seams towards centre front and centre back.
4 Cut ribbon shoulder-straps approximately 43cm (17in) long and pin to wrong side over front seams and 6mm (¼in) away from back

seams towards sides. Try slip on and adjust straps.
5 Pin right side of broderie anglaise edging to wrong side of slip top edge, placing join at side seam and making a small dart at centre front so that the edging will lie flat when turned to the right side. Stitch in place taking a 1.5cm (⅝in) seam. *See diagram 1.*

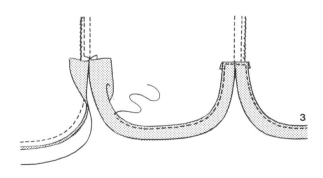

6 Trim seam allowance to 6mm (¼in) and press seam upward. Turn edging to right side and tack close to seam edge. On the right side, top stitch close to the top edge to hold the trim down. *See diagram 2.* Using small hand-stitches, catch the trim to the slip at seams to keep it flat. Press flat.

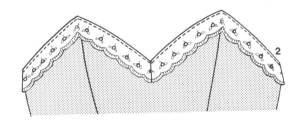

7 With right sides together, tack and stitch bias binding to the seamline of each hem section, leaving a turning each end of every strip. Trim seam allowance to 6mm (¼in). Turn binding to wrong side, turning in ends and tack. Stitch close to binding edge for hem. Press flat. *See diagram 3.*

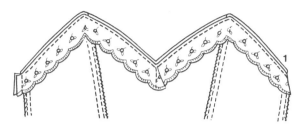

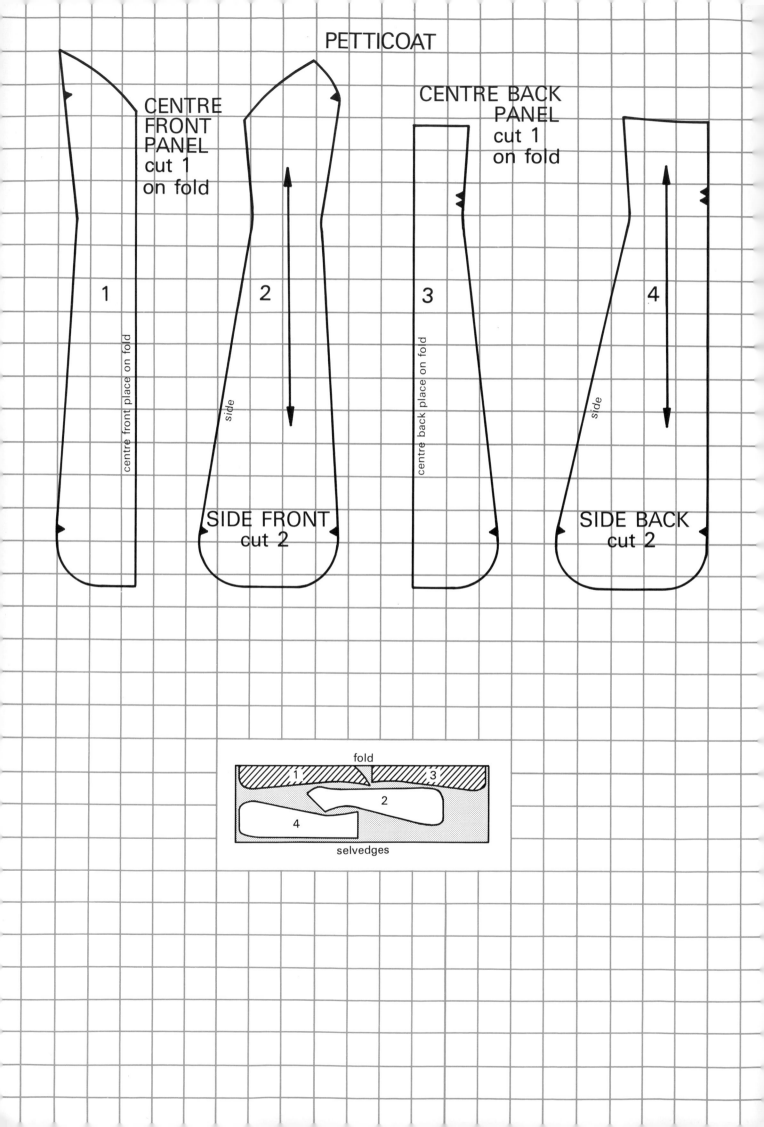

PETTICOAT

CENTRE
FRONT
PANEL
cut 1
on fold

1

centre front place on fold

CENTRE BACK
PANEL
cut 1
on fold

2

side

SIDE FRONT
cut 2

3

centre back place on fold

4

side

SIDE BACK
cut 2

fold

1   3

2

4

selvedges

Knitted camiknickers/Knitted teddy

Comfortable camiknickers/teddy knitted in a fine mercerised cotton. Narrow satin ribbon in a contrast colour is threaded through eyelet holes and drawn up to fit.

Materials
22[24:26] 20g balls of Twilleys Twenty; 1 pair of 2¼mm (No 13) knitting needles; 4m (4yd) of 6mm (¼in) wide ribbon; 80cm (32in) of 1.25cm (½in) wide ribbon.

Measurements
To fit bust 83[87:92]cm (32[34:36]in); length: 62[64:65]cm (24½[25:25½]in).
Note: Follow instructions in [ ] for larger sizes.
Tension: 20 sts to 5cm (2in).

Abbreviations
K = knit; p = purl; st(s) = stitch(es); st st = stocking stitch; beg = beginning; dec = decrease; inc = increase; mm = millimetres; cm = centimetres; in = inch(es).

Front
RIGHT LEG: Using yarn double throughout cast on 89[94:99] sts. Proceed in st st working 10 rows, ending with p row.
Eyelet-hole row 1: K4, (cast off 1st, k until there are 4 sts on right-hand needle after cast-off st) repeat ( ) to end.
Eyelet-hole row 2: P4, (cast on 1st, p4) repeat ( ) to end.
Continuing in st st, work 10 rows, ending with p row.
Inc 1 st at beg of next and every following alternate row to 95[100:105] sts. Purl 1 row.
To shape crotch: Dec 1 st at shaped edge on next 5 rows, then on every following alternate row to 87 [92:97] sts, then on every following 4th row until 82[87:92] sts remain. Purl 1 row.
Cut off yarn and leave sts on a spare needle.
LEFT LEG: Work as given for right leg, reversing shaping, but do not cut off yarn.
Next row: K to end, then on to same needle k the sts from spare needle, giving 164[174:184] sts.
★Work straight to 30[32:33]cm (12[12½:13]in) from cast-on edge, ending with p row, then work the 2 eyelet-hole rows again.
Work straight to 64[65:66]cm (25[25½:26]in) from cast-on edge, ending with p row, then work the 2 eyelet-hole rows again.
Work 6 rows, ending with p row.
Cast off.★

Back
LEFT LEG: Using yarn double throughout, cast on 105[110:115] sts. Proceeding in st st, inc 1 st at beg of 5th and every following alternate row to 108[113:118] sts. Purl 1 row.
Next row: Inc in first st, k2 (cast off 1 st, k until there are 4 sts on right-hand needle after cast-off st) repeat ( ) to end.
Next row: P4, (cast on 1, p4) repeat ( ) to end.
Continuing in st st, inc 1 st at beg of next and every following alternate row to 123[128:133] sts. Work 5 rows straight, ending with p row.
To shape crotch: Cast off 20 sts at beg of next row, giving 103[108:113] sts. Dec 1 st at shaped edge on every row to 93[98:103] sts, then on every following 4th row to 90[95:100] sts, then on every following alternate row until 87[92:97] sts remain. Work 3 rows straight, ending with p row. Cut off yarn and leave sts on a spare needle.
RIGHT LEG: Work as given for left leg, reversing shaping, but do not cut off yarn.
Next row: K to end, then on to same needle k the sts from spare needle, giving 174[184:194] sts.
Now work as given for front from ★ to ★.
TO COMPLETE: Pin out to size, then press with a hot iron over a damp cloth. Join side and inner-leg seams. Turn 6mm (¼in) to wrong side at top edge and slipstitch in position.
Finish legs in the same way.
Cut the 6mm (¼in) wide ribbon into 4 lengths and thread through eyelet-holes to tie. Cut the 1.25cm (½in) wide ribbon in half and sew to top at front and back to form straps, adjusting length as required.

Knitted bedjacket

A bedjacket you will love to wear. It is simply knitted in moss stitch throughout with garter stitch edges. It is decorated with fluffy pompons in two contrasting colours.

Materials
15[16:17] 25g balls Patons Trident DK; 2 10g balls of Patons Fuzzy Wuzzy in each of two contrasting colours for pompons. 1 pair of 3¾mm (No 9) long knitting needles; 2 4cm (1½in) diameter circles of card for each pompon.

Measurements
To fit bust 83[87:92]cm (32[34:36]in); length: 48[50:51]cm (19[19½:20]in); sleeve: 16.5cm (6½in).
Note: Follow instructions in [ ] for larger sizes.
Tension: 17sts to 7.5cm (3in) over m st.

Abbreviations
K = knit; p = purl; st(s) = stitch(es); m st = moss stitch; rep = repeat; beg = beginning; dec = decrease; inc = increase; mm = millimetres; cm = centimetres; in = inch(es).

LEFT FRONT:
Cast on 47[51:53] sts. K 12 rows; mark ridge of last row to denote right side.
M st row: K1 (p1, k1) to end.
Rep last row to 26.5cm (10½in) from cast-on edge, ending with right side.
To shape front edge: Dec 1 st at beg of next and every following 4th row until 29[31:33] sts remain.
Work straight until front measures 48[50:51]cm (19[19½:20]in) from cast-on edge, ending with wrong side.
To shape shoulders: Cast off 10 sts at beg of next and following alternate row. Work 1 row. Cast off.
RIGHT FRONT:
Work as given for left front reversing shaping.
BACK:
Cast on 101[107:113] sts. K 12 rows.
Proceed in m st until back is same length as fronts up to beg of shoulder shaping.
To shape shoulder: Cast off 10 sts at beg of next 4 rows and 9[11:13] sts at beg of following 2 rows. Cast off.
SLEEVES (*both alike*):
Cast on 81[85:89] sts.
K 12 rows.
Proceeding in m st, inc 1 st each end of every

following 6th row to 93[97:103] sts. Work straight to 16.5cm (6½in) from cast-on edge.
To shape top: Cast off 9 sts at beg of next 8[8:6] rows, and 8[9:10] sts at beg of following 2[2:4] rows. Cast off.
THE BORDER:
Join shoulder seams. With right side facing join yarn to lower edge of right front and k up 246 [253:260] sts evenly round front edge. K 10 rows. Cast off.
TO COMPLETE:
Do not press. Mark depth of armholes 21.5[23:24]cm (8½[9:9½]in) from shoulder seams on back and fronts. Sew sleeves to armholes between markers. Join side and sleeve seams. Following the diagrams make 8 pompons in first contrasting colour and 9 in second contrasting colour. *Diagram 1*. Holding the 2 card discs together, wind yarn through the hole in the centre until the hole is virtually filled. Then snip the yarn between the discs at the outer edge, tie a tight knot between the discs, remove discs and trim pompon. Sew on pompons, placing them as desired.

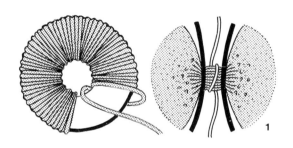

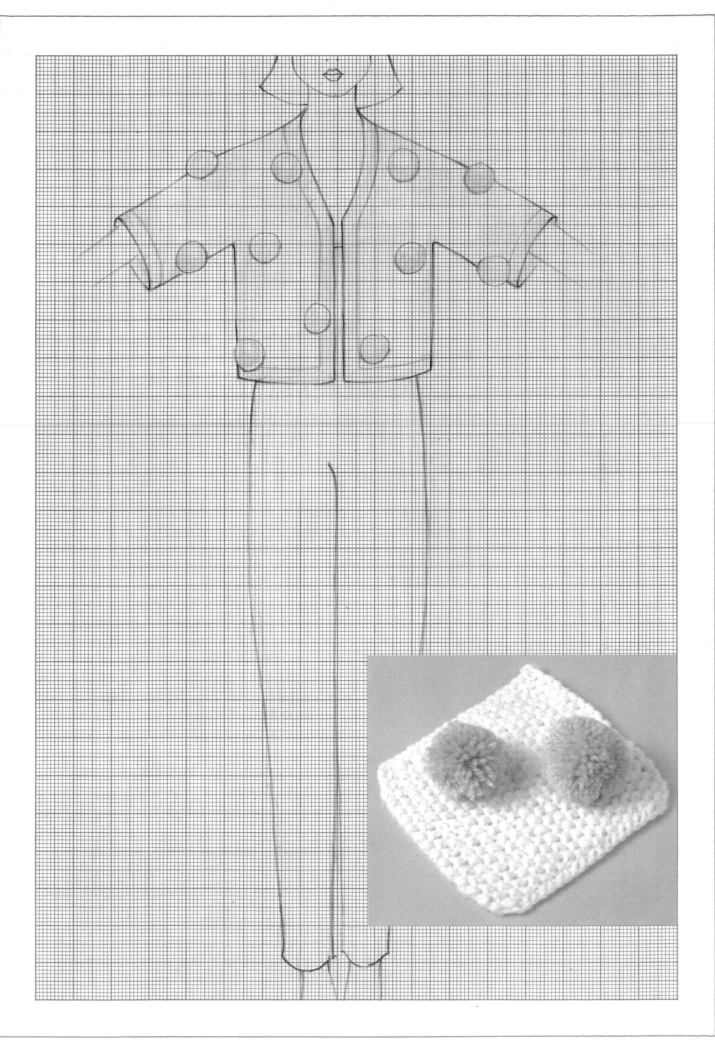

Keep cool and pretty in pure silk crêpe-de-chine richly trimmed with lace, so comfortable to wear.

Materials

1m (1⅛yd) of 115cm (45in) wide silk crêpe-de-chine

2.4m (3¾yd) of 4cm (1½in) wide scallop-edged nylon lace

3 buttons 6mm (¼in)

1.2m (1yd) of 6mm (¼in) wide satin ribbon

2 hooks and bars (size 0)

sewing thread to match fabric

squared paper for pattern

Measurements

The pattern is given in size 12, for measurements see chart on page 123.

To make pattern

Draw up the pattern to scale from the graph pattern given here. One square represents 2.5cm (1in).

To adapt pattern

For size 10, cut away 1.3cm (½in) from front and back side seams and from front and back bra-top side seams.

For size 14, alter in the same places but add amounts.

To cut out

No seam allowance is included on the pattern. When cutting out add 1.5cm (⅝in) to all edges. Pin pattern pieces to fabric following the cutting layouts and cut out. For centre-back opening cut a bias strip of fabric 2.5cm × 23cm (1in × 9in). Transfer all pattern markings.

To make the camiknickers

1 Overcast the side-seam edges of the camiknickers front and back.

2 Reinforce the centre-back opening by working a line of machine stitching 6mm (¼in) from centre-back top edge, tapering to a point at the lower edge of opening and working out to 6mm (¼in) at top of other side.

Slit opening to point and open out. Bind edge with bias strip taking 6mm (¼in) seam allowance. *See diagram 1.*

3 Reinforce the front and back crotch-gusset seams in the same way.

With right sides together, tack and stitch front and back crotch gussets in place. *See diagram 2.*

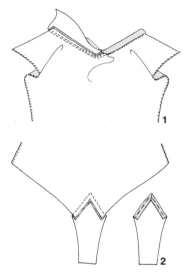

Turn under seam allowance on corresponding seam edges of gusset facings and tack. Press flat. With wrong sides together tack and slipstitch gusset facings to gusset seams. Tack raw edges of gussets and gusset facings together 1.5cm (⅝in) in. *See diagram 3.*

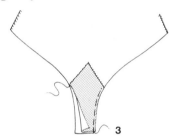

4 With right sides together, tack and stitch front to back at side seams. Press seams open.

5 With right sides together, tack and stitch the front bra sections together. Trim seam allowance to 6mm (¼in) and press towards side.

With wrong sides together, place two front bra sections together and tack all round 1.5cm (⅝in) in from all edges. Repeat for second two bra sections.

6 With right sides together tack and stitch two back sections together along top and centre-back edges only. Trim seam allowance and turn to right side. Press flat.

7 Pin lace in position on right side of front bra sections, matching straight edge to tacking line and balancing scalloped edge outwards, mitring the top point. *See diagram 4, and page 132 for instructions on mitring.*

Tack lace in position on the seam line not too close to the edge.

Stitch in place with a fine zigzag stitch on the straight edge of the lace. *See diagram 5.*

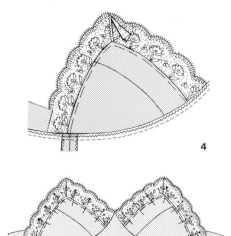

4

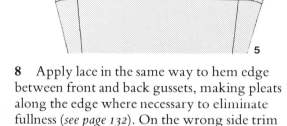

5

8 Apply lace in the same way to hem edge between front and back gussets, making pleats along the edge where necessary to eliminate fullness (*see page 132*). On the wrong side trim away excess fabric close to stitching.

9 Pin the lace sides of the front bra pieces to overlap the back bra pieces as indicated on the pattern. Zigzag stitch in place and neaten.

10 With right sides together, tack and stitch back bra sections to back from centre back to notch. Snip seam allowance at notch almost to line of stitching. Turn under seam allowance and slipstitch to stitching line.

With right sides together, tack and stitch the remainder of the bra back and front to the front and back. Work a second row of stitching 6mm ($\frac{1}{4}$in) away from the first. Trim excess fabric close to second row of stitching and overcast raw edges by machine. Press seam upwards.

11 With right sides together, tack and machine button and buttonhole sections to crotch raw edges. Turn under seam allowance on all raw edges, fold tab over and slipstitch to stitching line, and close short edges.

12 Work 3 buttonholes evenly spaced on back-crotch edge and sew buttons to correspond on front edge.

13 Sew ribbon straps to inside of points on bra fronts and to inside of back.

14 Sew hooks to right centre-back opening and bars on left to correspond.

15 Tie a small ribbon bow and sew it to the centre front.

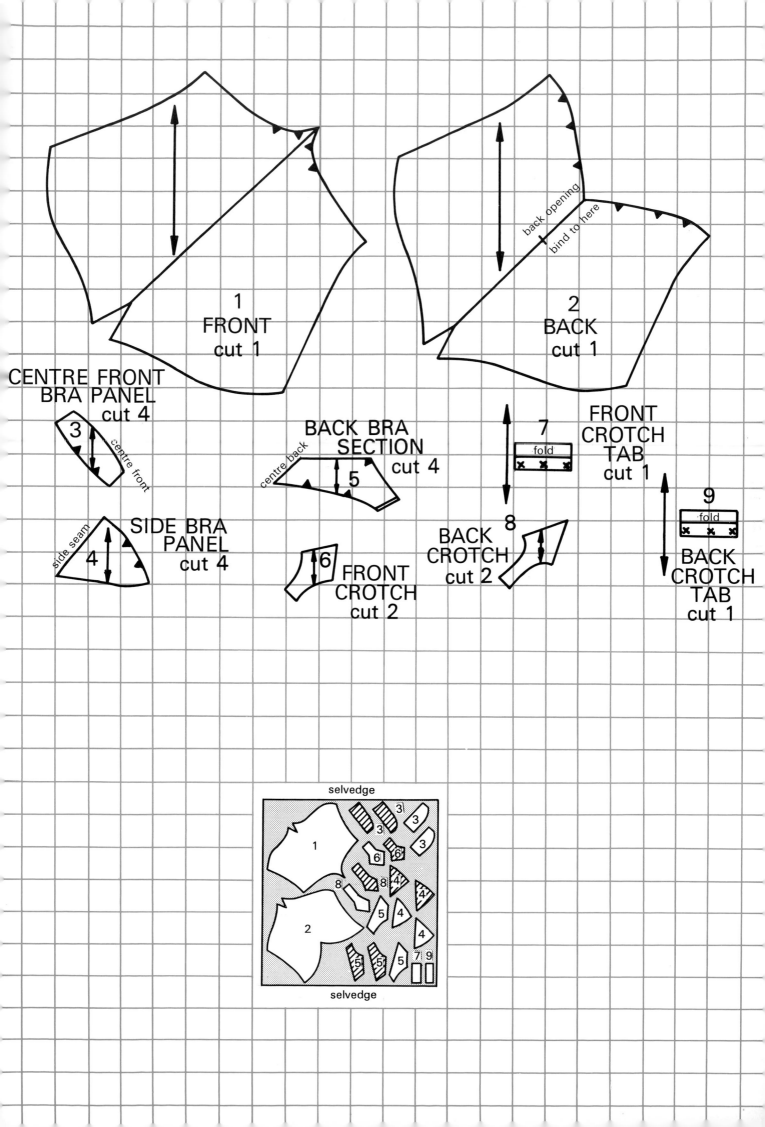

1
FRONT
cut 1

2
BACK
cut 1

back opening
bind to here

CENTRE FRONT
BRA PANEL
cut 4

3

centre front

BACK BRA
SECTION
cut 4

centre back

5

7
fold

FRONT
CROTCH
TAB
cut 1

8

9
fold

SIDE BRA
PANEL
cut 4

side seam

4

6

FRONT
CROTCH
cut 2

BACK
CROTCH
cut 2

BACK
CROTCH
TAB
cut 1

selvedge

1

3
3

3

6
6

8
8
4

2

5
4

4

5
5
5

7 9

selvedge

Lace bra & briefs

Keep cool and pretty in this dainty bra, brief and garter set made from a mere whisper of lace. They take so little fabric to make that you can really pamper yourself and indulge in the luxury of the most expensive lace.

Materials

40cm (½yd) of 115cm (45in) wide lace
30cm (1⅓yd) of 90cm (36in) wide crêpe-de-chine
70cm (¾yd) of 1cm (⅜in) wide loom elastic
1cm (⅜in) plastic bra fastener
80cm (31in) of 2cm (¾in) wide loom elastic
1.4m (1½yd) of 2.5cm (1in) wide satin ribbon
1.4m (1½yd) of 6mm (¼in) wide baby ribbon
2m (2¼yd) of 1cm (⅜in) wide lace trimming
1.5m (1⅔yd) of 6mm (¼in) wide knicker elastic
sewing thread to match fabric
squared paper for patterns

Measurements

The pattern is given in size 12, for measurements see chart on page 123.

To make pattern

Draw up the pattern to scale from the graph pattern given. One square represents 5cm (2in).

To adapt pattern

For size 10, cut away 1.3cm (½in) from side seams of briefs and 6mm (¼in) from front and side edges of bra.
For size 14, alter in the same places but add amounts.

To cut out

No seam allowance is included on the pattern. When cutting out add 1.5cm (⅝in) to all seam edges.
Pin pattern pieces to fabric following the cutting layout and cut out.
Transfer all pattern markings.

To make bra

1   Stitch darts in bra cups. Press darts to side and zigzag stitch close to seam. Trim seam allowance close to stitching.
2   Turn over 1.5cm (⅝in) at top edges of cups and tack.
3   Lay lace trimming just under folded edge and attach with a fine zigzag machine stitch. *See diagram 1.* Press flat. Trim away excess seam allowance close to stitching.
4   Turn up and tack seam allowance on lower edge.

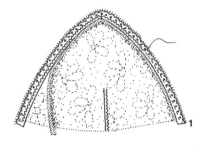

5   Cut 1cm (⅜in) wide loom elastic to required length to fit under bust plus 1.5cm (⅝in) seam allowance at each end.
6   Attach bra fastener to each end of elastic.
7   Mark centre front of elastic and on right side of material attach bra cups either side of this, pinning the side edge of each bra cup 17cm (6¾in) from the centre front and, stretching the elastic, pin remainder.
Machine with a wide zigzag stitch on top edge of elastic, stretching elastic as you do so. *See diagram 2.* Trim away excess seam allowance.

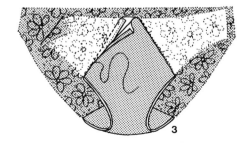

8   Tie a small baby-ribbon bow and stitch it to the centre front.
9   Attach baby-ribbon straps to fit, placing them at cup point and midway between side of cup and centre back.

To make briefs

1   With right sides together, tack and stitch crotch to front and back lace sections. Press seams towards crotch.
2   Turn under seam allowance on crotch facing at front and back seam edges and tack. Press flat. Pin crotch facing to wrong side of crotch and slip stitch to stitching line. *See diagram 3.* Press flat.

3 Tack lace trimming to seam line on right side around each leg and machine in place using a straight stitch. Place join of lace at back crotch seam. Press flat. Trim seam allowance to 6mm ($\frac{1}{4}$in).

4 Cut a strip of elastic approximately 44.5cm ($17\frac{1}{2}$in) for each leg. Attach by stretching and pinning; then machine using a fine zigzag stitch that spans the width of the elastic.

5 Turn over 6mm ($\frac{1}{4}$in) and 1cm ($\frac{3}{8}$in) on top edge of briefs. Stitch casing, leaving a small gap at centre back.

6 Cut a length of elastic to fit the waist comfortably plus 1.5cm ($\frac{1}{2}$in).
Using a bodkin, insert elastic in casing. Overlap ends by 1.5cm ($\frac{1}{2}$in) and sew securely together. Slipstitch opening to close.

7 Tie a small ribbon bow and stitch it to the centre-front top.

To make garters

1 Cut 2 pieces of 2cm ($\frac{3}{4}$in) wide elastic to measure 39cm ($15\frac{1}{2}$in) each. Overlap the ends 1.5cm ($\frac{5}{8}$in) to form circles and zigzag stitch to secure.

2 Cut 2 strips of 2.5cm (1in) wide ribbon measuring 66.5cm ($26\frac{1}{4}$in) each. Join ends to form circles.
Pin and stretch elastic to fit ribbon. Using a small zigzag stitch, machine ribbon to elastic 3mm ($\frac{1}{8}$in) in from each edge, stretching the elastic whilst doing so.

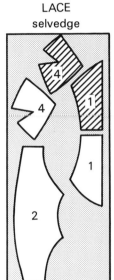

LACE
selvedge

selvedge

FABRIC
fold

selvedges

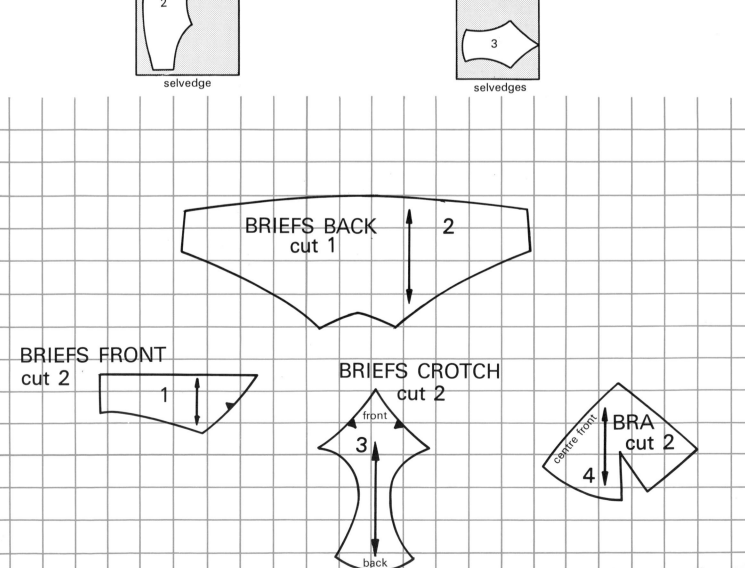

BRIEFS BACK
cut 1
2

BRIEFS FRONT
cut 2
1

BRIEFS CROTCH
cut 2

front

3

back

centre front

BRA
cut 2

4

Waist slip

A mere wisp of a slip made in the softest pure silk crêpe-de-chine. The hem and side slit edges are trimmed with dainty lace – simple enough for a beginner to make.

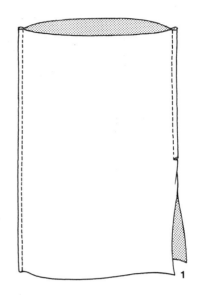

Materials

1.4m (1⅔yd) of 90cm (36in) wide fabric
2m (2¼yd) of 3.2cm (1¼in) wide lace edging
6mm (¼in) wide elastic for waist
sewing thread to match fabric
squared paper for pattern

Measurements

The pattern is given in size 12, for measurements see chart on page 123.

To make pattern

Draw up the pattern to scale from the graph pattern given here. One square represents 5cm (2in).

To adapt pattern

For size 10, pleat out 2.5cm (1in) from front and back pattern pieces.
For size 14, alter in the same places but add amounts.

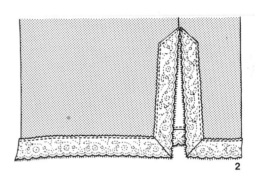

To cut out

No seam allowance is included on the pattern. When cutting out add 1.5cm (⅝in) to seam and hem edges, and 2cm (¾in) to waist edge.
Transfer all pattern markings.

To make the slip

1   Using french seams, stitch right-side seam and left-side seam from waist edge to dot. Clip to dot. Press seams towards back. *See diagram 1.*
2   Turn seam allowance to wrong side on slit and hem edges and tack close to fold edge. Turn under 6mm (¼in) on raw edge and machine stitch hem.
3   Tack lace edging to slit and hem edges, mitring at corners and turning under raw edges. On the right side, top stitch in place. *See diagram 2.*
4   At waist edge turn under 6mm (¼in) and then a further 1.3cm (½in).
Tack and machine, leaving an opening for threading elastic.
Cut a piece of elastic to fit the waist comfortably plus 1.3cm (½in). Thread elastic through waist casing. Overlap ends and sew together securely. Slipstitch opening to close.

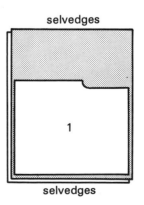

selvedges

selvedges

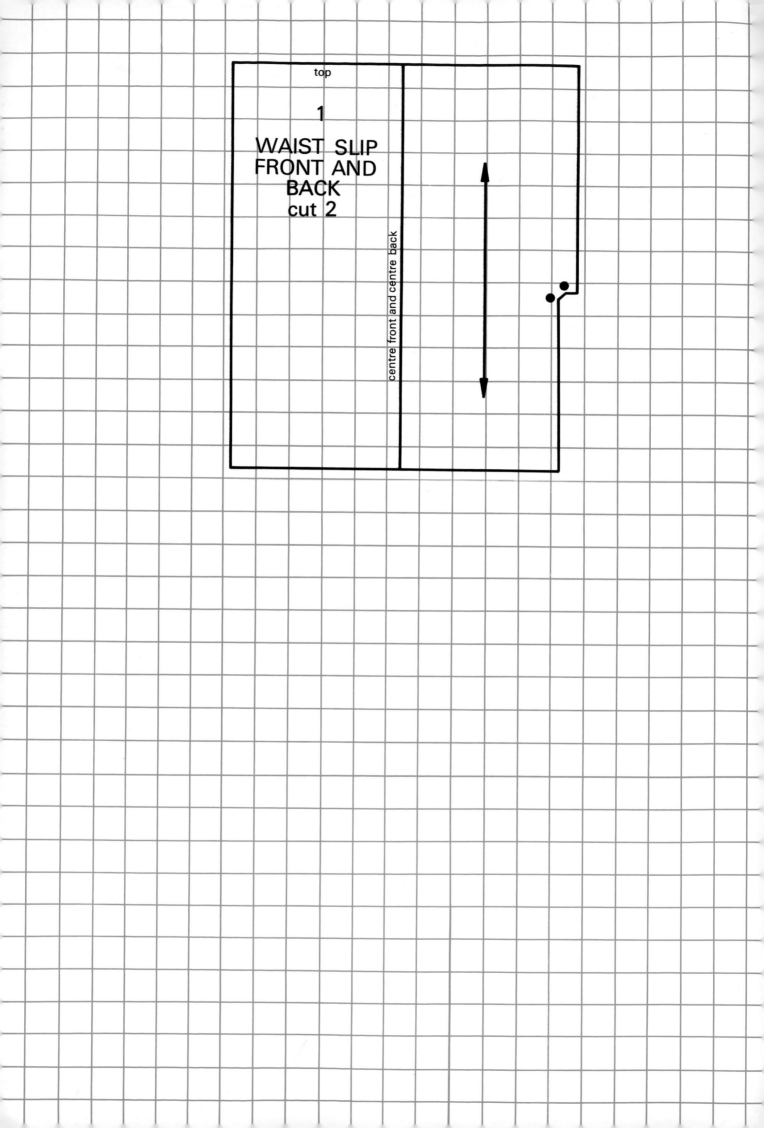

top

1

WAIST SLIP
FRONT AND
BACK
cut 2

centre front and centre back

Dressmaking techniques

Body size and fabric tables   123
Metric conversion table   123
Making patterns from a diagram   124
Types of seam   125
Seam finishes   126
Machine stitches   127
Hand stitches   128
Setting in sleeves   129
Hems   130
Rouleau   131
Applying lace   131
Buttonholes   132
Belt carriers   133
Problem fabrics   134
Pressing   134

Dressmaking techniques

In this chapter we give detailed instructions on the techniques mentioned in the making of the garments throughout the book. There is information on how to draw the graph patterns up to full size and helpful tips to help the beginner perfect her sewing techniques, whilst at the same time acting as a useful reminder to the more experienced dressmaker.

In dressmaking, it is the care and attention to detail that produces professional results and the following tips are aimed to help you achieve perfect results every time.

Fabric Widths

cm	in
90	35–36
115	44–45
150	58–60

Body size and fabric tables

Measurement Chart						
SIZE		10	12	14	16	18
Bust	cm	83	87	92	97	102
	in	$32\frac{1}{2}$	34	36	38	40
Waist	cm	64	67	71	76	81
	in	25	$26\frac{1}{2}$	28	30	32
Hip	cm	88	92	97	102	107
	in	$34\frac{1}{2}$	36	38	40	$42\frac{1}{2}$
Back waist length	cm	40.5	41.5	42	42.5	43
	in	$15\frac{3}{4}$	16	$16\frac{1}{4}$	$16\frac{1}{2}$	$16\frac{3}{8}$

Metric conversion table   *Conversions from a metre upwards are rounded to the nearest inch*

mm	in				m	yd		m	yd
3	$\frac{1}{8}$	8	$3\frac{1}{8}$		1.7	$1\frac{3}{4}+4$in		3.9	$4\frac{1}{4}+1$in
6	$\frac{1}{4}$	8.3	$3\frac{1}{4}$		1.8	$2\ -1$in		4.0	$4\frac{1}{4}+4$in
cm	**in**	8.5	$3\frac{3}{8}$		1.9	$2\ +3$in		4.1	$4\frac{1}{2}-1$in
1	$\frac{3}{8}$	8.9	$3\frac{1}{2}$		2.0	$2\frac{1}{4}-2$in		4.2	$4\frac{1}{2}+3$in
1.3	$\frac{1}{2}$	9.5	$3\frac{3}{4}$		2.1	$2\frac{1}{4}+2$in		4.3	$4\frac{3}{4}-2$in
1.5	$\frac{5}{8}$	**cm**	**yd**		2.2	$2\frac{1}{2}-3$in		4.4	$4\frac{3}{4}+2$in
2	$\frac{3}{4}$	10	$\frac{1}{8}-\frac{1}{2}$in		2.3	$2\frac{1}{2}+1$in		4.5	$5\ -3$in
2.5	1	20	$\frac{1}{4}-1$in		2.4	$2\frac{1}{2}+4$in		4.6	$5\ +1$in
3	$1\frac{1}{8}$	30	$\frac{3}{8}-1\frac{1}{2}$in		2.5	$2\frac{3}{4}-1$in		4.7	$5\frac{1}{4}-4$in
3.2	$1\frac{1}{4}$	40	$\frac{3}{8}+2$in		2.6	$2\frac{3}{4}+3$in		4.8	$5\frac{1}{4}$
3.5	$1\frac{3}{8}$	50	$\frac{1}{2}+1\frac{1}{2}$in		2.7	$3\ -2$in		4.9	$5\frac{1}{4}+4$in
3.8	$1\frac{1}{2}$	60	$\frac{5}{8}+1$in		2.8	$3\ +2$in		5.0	$5\frac{1}{2}-1$in
4.2	$1\frac{5}{8}$	70	$\frac{3}{4}+\frac{1}{2}$in		2.9	$3\frac{1}{4}-3$in		5.5	$6\ +1$in
4.5	$1\frac{3}{4}$	80	$\frac{7}{8}$		3.0	$3\frac{1}{4}+1$in		6.0	$6\frac{1}{2}+2$in
5	2	90	$1\ -\frac{1}{2}$in		3.1	$3\frac{1}{2}-4$in		6.5	$7\ +4$in
5.3	$2\frac{1}{8}$	**m**	**yd**		3.2	$3\frac{1}{2}$		7.0	$7\frac{3}{4}-3$in
5.7	$2\frac{1}{4}$	1.0	$1\ +3$in		3.3	$3\frac{1}{2}+4$in		7.5	$8\frac{1}{4}-2$in
6	$2\frac{3}{8}$	1.1	$1\frac{1}{4}-2$in		3.4	$3\frac{3}{4}-1$in		8.0	$8\frac{3}{4}$
6.5	$2\frac{1}{2}$	1.2	$1\frac{1}{4}+2$in		3.5	$3\frac{3}{4}+3$in		8.5	$9\frac{1}{4}+2$in
6.7	$2\frac{5}{8}$	1.3	$1\frac{1}{2}-3$in		3.6	$4\ -2$in		9.0	$9\frac{3}{4}+3$in
7	$2\frac{3}{4}$	1.4	$1\frac{1}{2}+1$in		3.7	$4\ +2$in		9.5	$10\frac{1}{2}-4$in
7.6	3	1.5	$1\frac{3}{4}-4$in		3.8	$4\frac{1}{4}-3$in		10.0	$11\ -2$in
		1.6	$1\frac{3}{4}$						

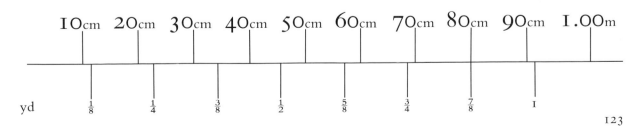

Making patterns from a diagram

Diagram patterns are the most usual method of presenting fashion ideas in magazines and books. They are scaled down to fit into a book page and you have to draw them up to full scale. Many people feel daunted by the prospect of enlarging these diagrams into patterns, but it is easier than it looks and you do not need any drawing skill.

EQUIPMENT
To make a pattern from a diagram you will need the following:
A large flat surface – table or even the floor
Dressmaker's squared paper or paper you have marked into squares yourself – wall-lining paper is inexpensive and ideal for this purpose
A metre or yard stick for drawing straight lines
A flexible ruler (Flexi-curve) for curves
Soft-leaded pencil – B or 2B
Rubber
Sellotape
Scissors

METHOD
1   Check that the diagram pattern is the one recommended for your size. Draw the pattern up to the size given and, for a smaller size, trim off the excess at places mentioned before cutting out in fabric. For a larger size, add the amounts when cutting out.
2   When using dressmaker's pattern paper always check the diagram scale before drawing the pattern up. Throughout this book each square represents 5cm (2in), but in other publications the scale may be different.
3   When drawing the pattern up to full size, always start with the largest pieces. Number the squares on the diagram and then number the squares on the dressmaker's pattern paper to correspond for each pattern piece. The majority of pattern pieces have all the required shaping detail in the top part and the lines simply extend

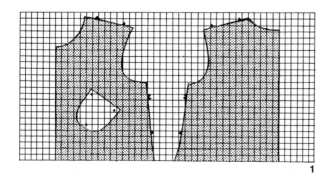

1

down to the required length. To save paper, draw up your patterns only as long as the paper sheet size will allow and then write clearly on the pattern how much needs to be added for the required finished length, including hem allowance. *See diagram 1.*
4   Commence by drawing up the straight lines on the pattern first. Notice where the lines on the diagram intersect a square and mark this in the same position on the dressmaker's squared paper at regular intervals. *See diagram 2.* Draw all the straight lines with a ruler and the curved ones with a Flexi-curve.

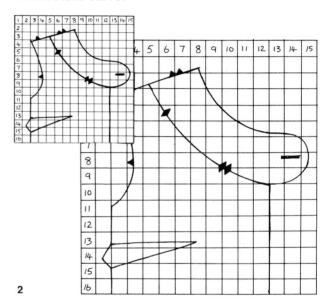

2

5   To save paper you can draw up the small pattern pieces inside the large ones. This is particularly useful for pockets, where you can draw and cut out the pocket pattern from the position in which it is to be sewn, making it easy to mark the pocket position on the fabric. *See diagram 1.*
6   On the pattern diagram you will notice a variety of markings such as grain line, notches and circles. All of these must be accurately marked onto the full-size pattern pieces and in turn transferred to the fabric after cutting out. These markings are essential information that you will need when making up the garment. Do not leave them off.
7   No seam or hem allowances are included on the patterns given in this book, so add the specified amounts stated for each pattern when cutting out the patterns.
8   Cut out the full-size pattern pieces and check the accuracy of your drawing by pinning the pieces together and checking the fitting.

9 Lay and pin all the pattern pieces onto the fabric as indicated on the cutting layout. If you have made a shortened version of the pattern, mark the extra length with pins or tailor's chalk on the fabric.

10 After cutting out, transfer all the pattern markings onto the fabric.

Types of seam

PLAIN SEAM

Place the fabric with right sides together, raw edges level, tack and stitch along the seamline with seam allowance as specified. Press the stitching line flat first to blend the stitches into the fabric, then press the seam open. *See diagram 3.*

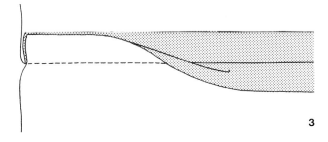

3

Trimming Trim seam allowances only where less bulk is required. An enclosed seam (for example inside a collar) is usually trimmed to 6mm ($\frac{1}{4}$in), but on very lightweight fabrics you may trim back a little more. Cut across corners diagonally, especially if they are to cross another seam. *See diagram 4.*

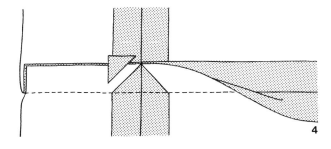

4

Grading Seams should be graded when they form an edge or are enclosed. The seam allowances are layered to different widths with the one lying next to the garment cut the widest, to give a smooth, flat edge. *See diagram 5.*

To trim a corner of an enclosed seam, cut the seam allowances across the point close to the stitching, then taper them on either side. *See diagram 6.*

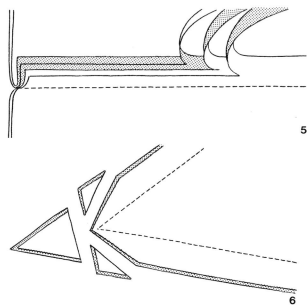

5

6

Notching and clipping On a curved seam, grade the seam allowance first. Then on an outward curve cut small notches from the seam allowance at regular intervals; on an inward curve, clip the seam allowance. Space the notches or clipping about 1.3cm to 2.5cm ($\frac{1}{2}$in to 1in) apart depending on the sharpness of the curve. Be careful not to cut the stitching. Always cut the notches from the seamline outwards. *See diagram 7.*

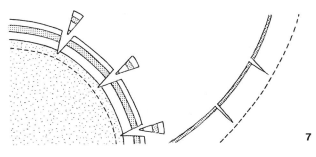

7

Finishing Some suitable methods of finishing a plain seam are: overcast by hand or machine, turned under and stitched and bound (see Seam Finishes, page 126).

FRENCH SEAM

This seam is used on fine and sheer fabrics and looks best if the finished width is 6mm ($\frac{1}{4}$in) or less.

With **wrong** sides together, tack and stitch the seam 1cm ($\frac{3}{8}$in) in from the raw edge. Trim seam allowance to 3mm ($\frac{1}{8}$in). With right sides together, crease along the stitched seam and press flat. Stitch along the seamline encasing the raw edges. *See diagram 8.*

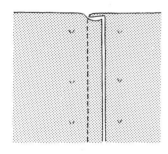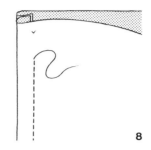

8

FLAT–FELL SEAM

With **wrong** sides together, tack and stitch a plain seam along the seamline. Press the seam towards one side. Trim the lower seam allowance to 3mm ($\frac{1}{8}$in). Turn under the top seam allowance 6mm ($\frac{1}{4}$in), tack and stitch close to folded edge. *See diagram 9.*

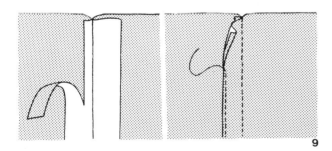

9

DOUBLE–STITCHED SEAM

Use this seam on lace and embroidered fabrics, or for curved seams on sheer fabrics. With right sides together, tack and stitch the seam on the seamline. Work a second row of stitching 3–6mm ($\frac{1}{8}$–$\frac{1}{4}$in) away in the seam allowance. Trim excess fabric close to second row of stitching and overcast the raw edge by hand or with a zigzag stitch on the machine. For sheer fabrics use machine embroidery cotton for the zigzag stitching. *See diagram 10.*

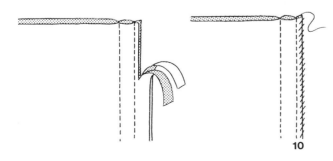

10

Seam finishes

The neatening of seam raw edges is a very important part in the making of any garment and should not be overlooked. A well neatened seam not only makes the garment look attractive on the wrong side but it helps it to wear longer and be laundered without the seam allowance fraying away. There are several methods that can be used to neaten raw edges but here we give the ones used in this book.

OVERCASTING (OVERSEWING) BY MACHINE

Most people nowadays own a swing-needle sewing machine and its zigzag stitch is a boon to home dressmakers, cutting down by hours the time spent on finishing seams.

When using the zigzag for neatening raw edges, place the raw edge to the centre of the machine foot and adjust zigzag to required depth of stitch on seam edge. Do not place raw edge up to where needle enters at right hand side of zigzag as this results in tight, hard edges and puckering. *See diagram 11.* On fine and sheer fabrics the neatening is more attractive and less noticeable if worked in machine embroidery cotton.

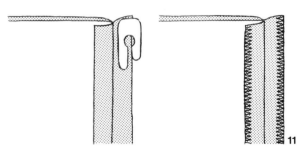

11

OVERCASTING (OVERSEWING) BY HAND

Before the introduction of the swing-needle sewing machine and zigzag stitch, this was the most used method of neatening raw edges. It is still very useful and gives a lighter touch than machine finishing on fine fabrics.

Work from left to right taking stitches 3mm ($\frac{1}{8}$in) deep and spaced at the same distance, making them slope over the raw edge. *See diagram 12.*

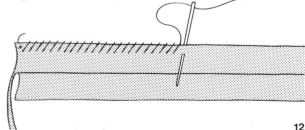

12

TURNED UNDER

Use this method for lightweight materials; it is not suitable for bulky or jersey fabrics. Working with the wrong side of the fabric uppermost, turn under 3mm ($\frac{1}{4}$in) on seam allowance edge and machine stitch. *See diagram 13.*

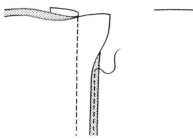

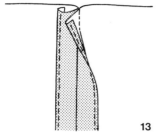

13

BOUND EDGES

This is a very strong and an attractive method of neatening raw edges. Purchased bias binding can be used, but it looks more attractive when done with self fabric or a fabric chosen especially for the purpose.

Cutting bias strips Take a rectangular piece of fabric cut on the straight of grain and fold it diagonally to find the true bias. Use the bias fold as a guide and mark the fabric with parallel lines spaced at the desired width of the bias strips (for a seam edge this would be 2.5–3.2cm [1–1$\frac{1}{4}$in] wide). *See diagram 14.*

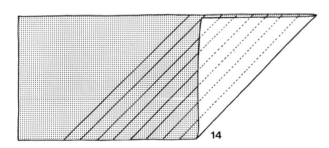

14

Joining bias strips Cut along the marking for the bias strips. The short ends cut on the grain will appear diagonal. Mark a seamline 6mm ($\frac{1}{4}$in) from each end. With right sides together, match the seamlines and not the cut edges, tack and stitch. Press the seam open and trim off the seam allowance level with the bias strip. *See diagram 15.*

Binding the edge With right sides together, tack and stitch the binding to the raw edge taking a 6mm ($\frac{1}{4}$in) seam allowance. *See diagram 16.* Turn under 6mm ($\frac{1}{4}$in) seam allowance on remaining

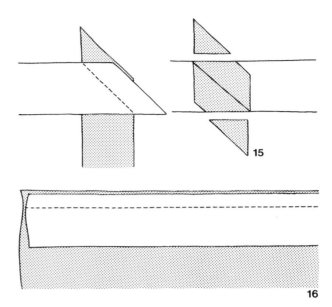

15

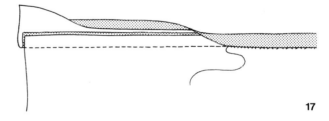

16

raw edge of binding and press. Fold the binding over the raw edge of garment or seam allowance enclosing it and, on the wrong side, slipstitch or hem to the line of stitching. *See diagram 17.*

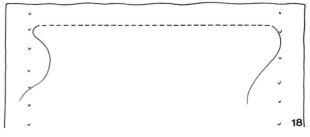

17

Machine stitches

The following are the stitches used in the construction and decoration of the garments in this book.

STAY STITCH

Before pinning, tacking and permanent stitching, curved areas should be stay stitched to prevent stretching out of shape whilst being handled. Simply work a row of machine stitching 3mm ($\frac{1}{8}$in) away from the seamline on the seam allowance, using the usual stitch length suited to your fabric. *See diagram 18.*

18

TOP STITCH

Top stitching can be used both as part of the construction of a garment and as a form of decoration. We have only used it as a part of the construction, to hold edges and sections of the garment firmly in the required position. Use the regular stitch tension and length suited to your fabric and machine, at the specified distance from the seam or garment edge.

GATHERING STITCHES

These can be worked by hand but are more easily controlled if worked on the sewing machine.
Set the stitch knob to the longest setting. Work one row of stitches 3 mm ($\frac{1}{8}$ in) either side of the seamline. See diagram 19. (With American patterns, the rows of gathering stitches are worked on and within the seamline.) Pull up the gathers on both threads at the same time to the required length. Tie a knot in thread ends and cut off excess. Pin the gathering to the flat piece it is to be joined to with the pins inserted on the seamline vertically. Always distribute the gathers evenly. You can machine directly over the pins as these do control the fabric well; or you tack and stitch in the usual way. See diagram 20.

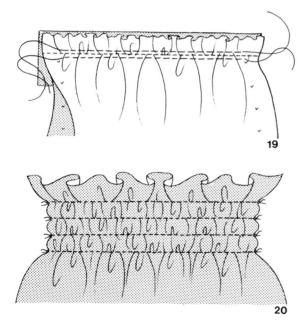

19

20

SHIRRING

Elasticised shirring is used to gather fabric to fit comfortably at waist, wrist, ankle and neck edges.
Wind the shirring elastic onto the machine bobbin by hand, stretching it slightly. Set the machine to a long stitch of about 7 stitches to 2.5 cm (1 in). Test the shirring on a piece of the garment fabric and adjust the tension if necessary.
On the garment, stitch on the right side as indicated on the pattern, stretching the fabric taut as you do so. You can use the previous row as a guide in conjunction with pattern markings to keep the rows straight. Keep each row taut as you stitch it. Finish ends off securely.

Hand stitches

Although much of the stitching of a garment can be done on the sewing machine, there are certain places where hand stitching is either essential or makes a more attractive finish.

Ordinary tacking (basting) Tacking stitches are not only used to hold the fabric together prior to stitching, but are vital in holding and controlling areas whilst pressing them. For example when you turn a collar or a facing to the right side after stitching, you need to tack close to the edges to hold it in shape for correct pressing.
Commence the stitching at the right-hand side by working a double back stitch and then, for seams, make the stitches about 1.3 cm ($\frac{1}{2}$ in) long and the spaces 3 mm ($\frac{1}{4}$ in). For tacking around edges take stitches of even length about 1 cm ($\frac{3}{8}$ in) each. Finish off stitching with a double back stitch. See diagram 21.
It is advisable to avoid tacking silk if possible as this leaves needle holes in the fabric when the stitches are removed.

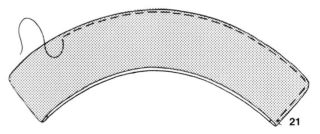

21

Basting (diagonal tacking) This stitch is used to hold two or more layers of fabric together as, for example, in quilting.
Take a horizontal stitch through all fabric layers about 1.3 cm ($\frac{1}{2}$ in) in length, depending on the thickness of the fabrics. Repeat directly below, placing stitches at approximately 7.5 cm (3 in) intervals. Do not pull the stitches tight. Work in rows from the centre outwards at 7.5–10 cm (3–4 in) intervals. See diagram 22.

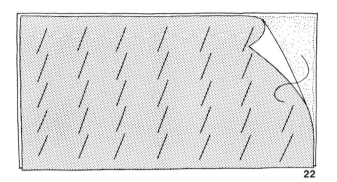

22

Hemming stitch This stitch is worked from right to left. Take a tiny stitch in the garment, picking up one thread of the fabric, then bring the needle up diagonally through the edge of the hem. Continue in this manner spacing the stitches 6mm ($\frac{1}{4}$in) apart. *See diagram 23.*

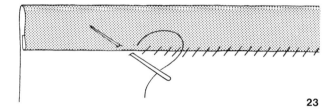

23

Slipstitch This stitch is used for hems, to attach linings, and to hold pockets and trimmings in place. The stitch is worked from right to left. Slide the needle through the folded edge for 3 to 6mm ($\frac{1}{8}$ to $\frac{1}{4}$ in); bring the needle out and, at the same point, pick up a thread of the under fabric or a stitch of the seamline. *See diagram 24.*

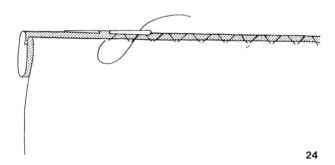

24

Setting in sleeves

The set-in sleeve in one style or another is the most popular sleeve shape in fashion, but one that the home dressmaker often finds difficult to handle. This is where it is so vital to transfer all the pattern markings onto the garment pieces after cutting out.

There are two methods of setting in a sleeve – the classic traditional way, and a modern easier method that is perfectly satisfactory for lingerie, casual wear and children's garments.

CLASSIC METHOD
Have the garment prepared with shoulder and side seams stitched.
1   Work 2 rows of gathering stitches between the notches on the sleeve head. Stitch any elbow darts and stitch the sleeve underarm seam. *See diagram 25.*

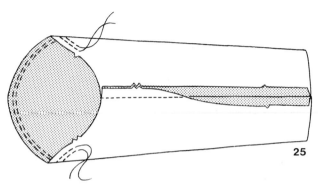

25

2   With right sides together, pin the sleeve into the armhole at underarm and shoulder seams and at notches, matching all the pattern markings correctly. Pull up the gathering threads to fit the sleeve head and tie ends to secure. Spread the gathers, or ease, evenly and pin with the pins lying vertical to the seamline. *See diagram 26.*

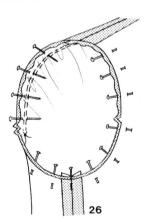

26

3   If there is too much 'ease' for it to be pinned out smoothly, you may have to unpin the sleeve from the armhole and shrink out the fullness using a steam iron, being careful not to shrink beyond the seamline.
4   With right sides together – matching underarm seams, circle to shoulder seam, and notches – pin the sleeve back into the armhole.

With the sleeve uppermost, stitch, commencing and finishing at the underarm seam. *See diagram 27.*

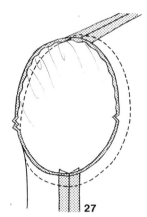

5 Do not press the armhole edges of a set-in sleeve, simply push them towards the sleeve. To neaten armhole raw edges, overcast by hand or machine. On cotton and similar weight fabrics you can neaten the seam raw edge by working a second row of stitching the width of the machine foot away from the first into the seam allowance. Trim excess fabric close to stitching and overcast by hand or machine.

EASY METHOD

With this method stitch the shoulder seams of the garment but leave the side seams open and do not stitch the underarm seam of the sleeve.
1 Work 2 rows of gathering stitches between the notches on the sleeve head.
2 With right sides together – matching underarm edges, notches, and circle to shoulder seam – pin the sleeve into the armhole. If necessary shrink excess 'ease' out as for classic method.
3 With the sleeve uppermost, stitch the seam. *See diagram 28.* Neaten raw edges as above.

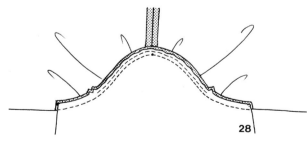

4 With right sides together, matching armhole seams, tack and stitch the side and underarm seams in one action. *See diagram 29.*

130

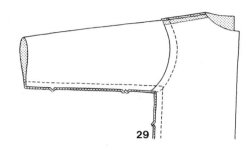

Hems

Hems are used to neaten the lower and outer edges of a garment. They should be carefully, accurately and neatly worked as a complimentary finish to the rest of the garment. As is done with seam allowances, the raw edges on hems must be neatened to prevent fraying in wear. The general rule is that the same method of neatening is used throughout the entire garment, but often this is not possible in the case of a hem as the least obtrusive method must be used.

BASIC PREPARATION

1 It is important that the hem should be of the right length and be parallel to the ground all round. So, get someone to measure and mark the hemline for you using a metre (yard) stick and pins or tailor's chalk.
2 With the right side of the garment facing you, turn up the hem on the marked line and tack close to the folded edge. *See diagram 30.*

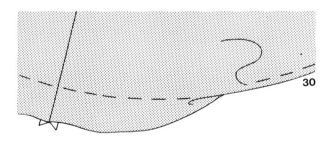

NARROW HEM

Trim the hem allowance to the required depth plus a 6mm to 1cm ($\frac{1}{4}$in to $\frac{3}{8}$in) turning. Turn under turning, tack and machine through all thicknesses or slipstitch by hand. *See diagram 31.*

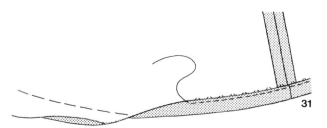

STITCHED AND OVERCAST

Trim hem allowance to the required depth. Work a row of straight machine stitching 3–6mm ($\frac{1}{8}$–$\frac{1}{4}$in) away from raw edge. Overcast raw edge by hand or machine. To ensure an invisible hem, turn back the edge 6mm ($\frac{1}{4}$in) and blind hem or catch stitch. *See diagram 32.*

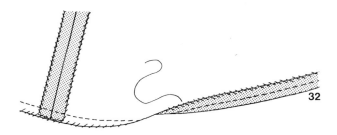

ROLLED HEM

For a rolled hem omit step 2 of the basic preparation.

Machine stitch 6mm ($\frac{1}{4}$in) below hemline. Trim hem allowance 3mm ($\frac{1}{8}$in) below stitching. *See diagram 33.*

Turn hem to the wrong side and roll a small section at a time between the finger and thumb of the left hand. Working from left to right, take a small slipstitch through the fold then, 3mm ($\frac{1}{8}$in) below that, pick up one or two threads of the fabric. Pull up thread to roll hem to wrong side. *See diagram 33.*

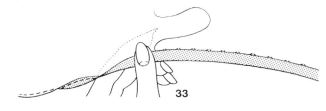

Rouleau

1 Cut a bias strip the desired length and double the finished width plus sufficient seam allowance to fill the tubing. (*See page 127* for instructions on how to cut a bias strip.) The width of the seam allowance depends on the thickness of the fabric – the finer the fabric, the wider the seam allowances. Work a test-piece on your fabric before making the final rouleau.

2 With right sides together, fold the bias lengthwise and stitch, stretching the fabric as you sew. At the end, slant the stitching to make the tube wider. *See diagram 34.*

To turn to right side, thread stitching-thread ends through the eye of a bodkin, securing them to the seam allowance so that they will not come

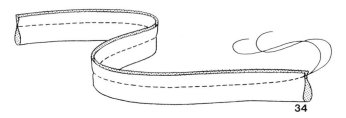

undone. Turn tubing to right side. *See diagram 35.*

It is not always necessary to finish off the ends but, if you have to do so, use a needle to tuck in the raw edge of the tube and catch it to hold with a few slipstitches.

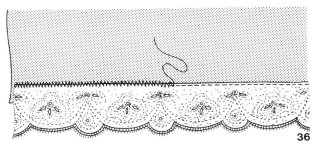

Applying lace

Lace always gives such a charming and feminine trim to lingerie. When applied by hand it takes hours to work tiny whip stitches, but with a zigzag stitch on the machine it is done in a few minutes.

1 Place the wrong side of the straight edge of the lace to the seamline on right side of fabric and tack.

2 Using a straight stitch, machine the lace to the garment close to the straight edge. Set the machine to a narrow, close zigzag and stitch over the straight stitching and edge of lace. *See diagram 36.*

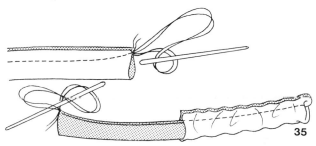

3 On the wrong side, using a pair of very sharp scissors, trim back excess seam allowance to stitching, being careful not to cut lace.

Note: You can simply zigzag stitch the lace onto the fabric but the above method is stronger.

On fine fabrics, the stitching looks more attractive if done in machine embroidery cotton.

Lace is often applied to curved or shaped edges, where it must be shaped to lie flat.

ON A CURVED EDGE

1 Pin the lace to the seamline as instructed above and lay the garment flat on a table. Pin out tiny darts where necessary until the lace lies flat. *See diagram 37.*

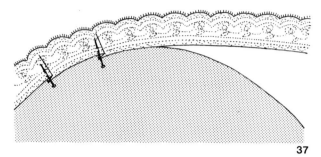

37

2 Unpin the lace and machine the darts. Work a second row of machining 3mm ($\frac{1}{8}$in) away from the first. Trim excess fabric close to stitching and whip stitch the raw edge by hand or overcast by machine. *See diagram 38.* Apply lace as above.

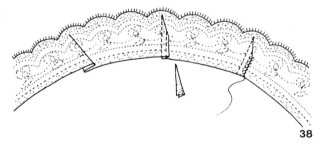

38

ON A SHAPED EDGE

On a shaped edge you will have to make tiny darts and make mitres at any corners too. It is helpful if you make a paper template to follow, using the garment pattern as a guide. To mitre a corner on lace:

1 Pin the lace to the garment to find where the mitre should be made. Measure to the outermost point where the corner point will be formed and mark with a pin. *See diagram 39.*

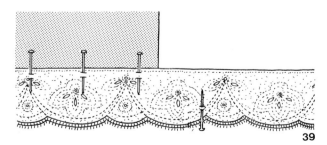

39

2 Remove the lace and fold it with right sides together at marked point. *See diagram 40.*

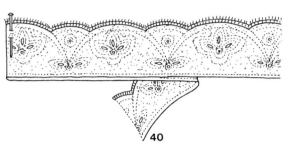

40

3 Turn the fold diagonally to meet the turned back edges of the lace and press. *See diagram 41.*

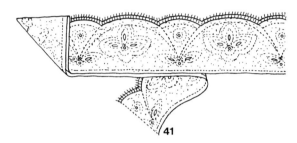

41

4 Open the fold and stitch along the pressed crease. Work a second row of stitching 3mm ($\frac{1}{8}$in) away from the first, trim back excess fabric and whip stitch raw edges by hand or overcast by machine.

Buttonholes

Most modern sewing machines have an automatic buttonholer included as one of the utility stitches; but for those who do not have one of these or who would prefer to work a neatly stitched handworked buttonhole, here is what you do.

KEYHOLE BUTTONHOLE

Before you ever attempt to work a buttonhole on a garment, always work a test one on the fabric you are using. This should be folded double and include any interfacing that is being used.

1 Mark the position and size of the buttonhole with tacking stitches. Tack all round the buttonhole 1cm ($\frac{3}{8}$in) from marking and through all thicknesses of fabric. *See diagram 42.*

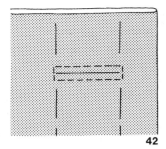

42

2 Using a pair of very sharp scissors (preferably buttonhole scissors), cut the buttonhole. With matching thread in the needle, overcast the buttonhole raw edges to prevent fraying whilst working. Make the stitches almost as deep as the buttonhole stitch will be and follow the grain of the fabric. *See diagram 43.*

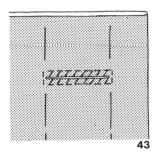

43

3 With a 90cm (36in)-long single thread in the needle, secure the thread with a couple of tiny back stitches to the wrong side of the inner bottom edge of the buttonhole. Bring the needle to the right side and work buttonhole stitch as shown along one side. *See diagram 44.* When you

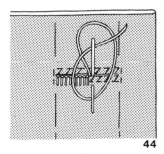

44

get to the end, work about 7 overcasting stitches closely together, turning the end as you do so. This is the part of the buttonhole that is going to take all the strain in wear, so be sure to take sufficient stitches round the end to make it strong. *See diagram 45.*
4 Work buttonhole stitch back along the remaining side. When you get to the end, work 4 straight stitches across the width of the entire buttonhole. Bring the needle up on the left-hand

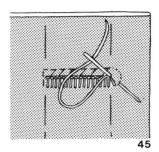

45

side of these stitches and work buttonhole stitch over them, catching the fabric underneath to make the buttonhole bar tack. *See diagram 46.*

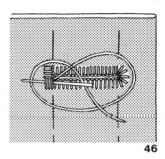

46

Take needle to back of work and finish off with a couple of back stitches.
This keyhole buttonhole is worked horizontally. For buttonholes worked vertically, finish with a bar tack at each end. The bar tacks are worked after the main part of the buttonhole.

Belt carriers
Belt carriers are used to help hold the belt in the correct place on the garment both in wear and off. They can be made in self fabric but, for lingerie wear, crochet- or buttonhole-stitch carriers are more delicate.

CROCHET CARRIER
Securely attach one end of a length of sewing thread to the position indicated on the pattern for the belt carrier. Using a fine crochet hook work chain stitch to the required length. *See diagram 47.* Sew end of chain stitch securely to second marking for carrier.

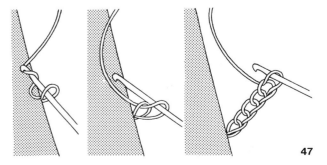

47

BUTTONHOLE-STITCH CARRIER
Thread a needle with a long length of sewing
thread and work a foundation-bar of several
threads between the belt-carrier position
markings as indicated on the pattern. These can
be worked over a ruler or some other rigid
object to keep them even in length. Then
buttonhole stitch over this bar for the entire
length. *See diagram 48.*

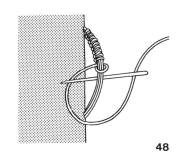

48

Problem fabrics
Every fabric has to be made up using the
techniques best suited to it, and some fabrics need
special handling to get perfect results. Many
modern sewing machines are designed to cater
for such materials, so if you have one of these
machines you should have less problems in
sewing fabrics such as stretch towelling and
sheers.

STRETCH TOWELLING/STRETCH TERRY
As its name implies, this is a stretch fabric, and
any stitching needs to have stretch built into it too.
If you have a stretch stitch on your machine, use
this. If not, set your machine to a short stitch and
a very slight zigzag. Practise on a scrap of your
fabric folded double until you get the correct
stitch. Test for this by pulling the stitching until
you achieve a seam that does not snap. If the
threads of the fabric snag as you stitch, use a ball-
point needle both in the machine and for hand
sewing.
In areas where stretch is undesirable – such as at
shoulders or crotch – seams must be stabilised
with tape. Press lightly to avoid stretching.

FINE FABRICS
Fine fabrics such as silk or polyester crêpe-de-
chine need to be stitched with pure silk thread or
mercerised cotton No 50, and a stitch length of
15–20 per 2.5cm (1in).
Enclosed seams such as french or flat-fell give a
neat and strong finish, but plain seams are

perfectly acceptable. Should the seam tend to
pucker even after careful tension adjustment,
place strips of tissue paper under the seam whilst
stitching. Tear paper away after seam has been
completed. Use machine embroidery cotton for
neatening seam raw edges by zigzag stitch.
Should this method of neatening result in
puckering, oversew by hand.

Pressing
Pressing is an essential technique in dressmaking.
It is used to flatten and shape seams, darts and
other stitched areas as they are sewn. Set up your
iron and ironing board near to your sewing
machine and use it at every stage of construction.
You must press each seam as you stitch it and not
leave all the pressing until the end. The
important thing to bear in mind is that pressing is
not ironing. Pressing is the process of lifting and
setting down the iron in the correct position.

BASIC EQUIPMENT
Iron Many people prefer a steam iron but a dry
iron is quite adequate. The important thing is
that, for dressmaking purposes, it should be
lightweight.

Ironing board An adjustable one that can be set at
varying heights is an advantage. It is best to get
one that has a metal cradle to hold the iron.

Sleeve board A sleeve board is an essential piece of
equipment and one that attaches firmly to the
ironing board is an advantage.

Pressing cloth A pressing cloth is used to apply
moisture, and to protect your fabric from the
heat of the iron; the fabric used for it depends
upon the material it is to be used on. For fine and
sheer fabrics use organdie; for cottons use a fine
lawn. Wash the fabric well to remove any
dressing before using it for a pressing cloth.
If the instructions indicate that pressing should be
done over a damp cloth, this does not mean a wet
one. Dip the pressing cloth in tepid water and
wring out well. Fold into quarters and pat with
the iron to eliminate excess moisture before
using.

BASIC RULES
1   Always test a scrap of your fabric to
determine the best temperature and technique.
Test a piece large enough so that you can
compare the pressed to the unpressed portion.

2 Whenever possible press *with* the grain of the fabric and be careful not to stretch edges or curves by pulling the material.

3 Whenever possible, press on the wrong side of the fabric. If you have to press on the right side, use a dry pressing cloth.

4 To prevent impressions of seam allowances or darts from showing on the right side of the fabric, place brown-paper strips under them. Cut the strips at least 5cm (2in) wider than the area that is to be pressed.

5 Try to use only the tip of the iron and work in the same direction as the stitching.

6 To avoid marking fabric, do not press over pins.

7 Most important of all, set your iron to the correct temperature for your fabric and do not overpress.